MY NEW NORMAL

THE UNSEEN

LIVI DEANE

My New Normal

Learning to celebrate what's different about you

First published in Great Britain in 2024

Society for Promoting Christian Knowledge
The Record Hall, 16–16A Baldwins Gardens
London EC1N 7RJ
www.spck.org.uk

British Library Cataloguing-in-Publication Data
A catalogue record for this book is available from the British Library

Hardback ISBN 978–0–281–08807–2
Paperback ISBN 978–0–281–08808–9
eBook ISBN 978–0–281–08809–6
audio ISBN 978–0–281–08810–2

1 3 5 7 9 10 8 6 4 2

Typeset by Fakenham Prepress Solutions
First printed in Great Britain by Clays Limited
Subsequently digitally printed in Great Britain
eBook by Fakenham Prepress Solutions

Produced on paper from sustainable forests

Contents

Foreword by Katie Piper OBE   vi

Prologue   viii

1 The beginning   1

2 Happy families   6

3 A class act   12

4 Pre-teen dream   17

5 Teen nightmare   21

6 Growing pains   29

7 Bad hair days   36

8 The rollercoaster   44

9 Facing my fears   51

10 The eye of the storm   55

11 Round two   59

12 The darkest nights   64

13 A fresh pair of eyes   68

14 My new normal   73

15 Looking for love   80

16 Becoming an influencer   87

17 A new career path   94

18 Living life to the max   98

19 Mum life   101

20 On the positive side...   108

Acknowledgements   110

Foreword

Everyone needs a friend like Livi Deane. She is a woman who knows what it is to suffer, to struggle and to overcome. If you're in a difficult place, you won't get any false platitudes from Livi, but instead a recognition of your pain and the steadfast support we all need.

That mentality comes through in every chapter of *My New Normal*. This is a story of a girl who was faced with a terrifying diagnosis yet still found hope for the future. We can all learn from the way she, even as a young girl, managed to respond with pragmatism, disappointment and optimism in equal parts.

I first came across Livi on social media, when she bravely shared photos of herself without her prosthetic eye. When I initially saw snippets of her story, I thought her eye had been removed after an accident. It was only when I watched a mini documentary about her journey that I realised the extent of her illness and the years of painful treatment she had been forced to endure.

I sent her a message to say that I loved what she had shared and to encourage her to keep speaking out. I also took the opportunity to compliment her fashion sense! We got chatting, and not long after I invited her to join me on my podcast, *Katie Piper's Extraordinary People*.

I couldn't help but be inspired by the resilience Livi showed when she spoke about her story. She models acceptance beautifully. She doesn't wallow, but takes the challenges in her stride and gets on with it. That's my kind of woman! I know better than most the vulnerability of showing your true self, flaws and all, when the world says that nothing less than perfect will do. After my life and appearance were altered forever, I felt UnSeen and, at the tender age of twelve, Livi had to face the same feelings.

This isn't simply a story of a cancer diagnosis. This is the story of a woman who refuses to give up, refuses to hide and refuses to let the world squash her spirit. She's faced trolls, cruel jokes and criticism, but she also knows her worth and value in a way we can all learn from. That doesn't mean it comes easily to her, but it does mean she refuses to give up the fight.

I know that you won't be able to read this book without feeling empowered. I am especially keen for teenage girls to learn from Livi's wisdom. We were all self-conscious and desperate to look great and be liked in our school years. But Livi's down-to-earth voice helps to place those desires in the context of what is really important.

This isn't just Livi's story. It's also that of her mum, who fasted with her before operations. It's that of her dad, who has been amazing through her illness, always ready to make her laugh. And of her stepdad, who has been so good to Livi and the rest of the family. It's the story of her nan, who prayed for a miracle over her body when doctors told them to say goodbye. It's that of her grandad, driving her to London for every hospital appointment because she felt too sick on the train. It's the party her friends threw her when she got the all-clear. It's her partner, who finds her just as attractive without her prosthetic eye. It's their little baby Kaito, who will grow up to know that his mum is a superwoman.

I am so proud that Livi's book is the third in my series, The UnSeen. Stories of overcoming and radical self-acceptance help us all to take a step further towards loving ourselves. If Livi can proudly show herself without her prosthetic eye, then why can't we show ourselves with all our beautiful differences? I hope, like me, you will learn that, even when the most difficult trials come, you are strong enough to overcome. We can't control what storms will hit, but we can accept and embrace our new normal.

Katie Piper OBE

Prologue

My song was 'Brown Eyed Girl' by Van Morrison. Both my sisters had deep-brown eyes but mine were different. They were a chestnut colour with flecks of hazel; unique and striking in their own way. I think that's why the first technician struggled to match my eye colour. Brown irises are supposed to be the easiest to paint onto a prosthetic eye but when I first put mine in, I felt hideous.

The shape was wrong. It looked bulbous in the socket. It wasn't just slightly lazy-looking, which was to be expected – it looked gruesome. It didn't have the subtle shades of chocolate that we, and Van Morrison, had spent years singing about. It was lighter and with no texture. My eyes didn't match.

I looked in the mirror, turning my face to get a full scope of vision from my one remaining eye. That's when I knew everything was not going to be OK. I'd kept positive. I'd taken every hit that had come my way. I'd made the best of the hair loss with bandannas and quirky haircuts. I'd ridden out the nausea and exhaustion of chemotherapy. I'd force-fed myself when food was the last thing I wanted. I'd endured it all because I was told that it was the only way to keep my eye.

And now it was gone anyway.

I'd had to undergo the dreaded surgery, and now I was a gaunt fourteen-year-old girl with a centimetre of hair and a crater on her face that could only be covered by an acrylic eye so comically fake-looking, it wouldn't have been out of place on Wednesday Adams.

I came home from the hospital in the first week of 2012. They'd let me keep my eye for one last Christmas before it had to be removed; a festive favour that didn't feel like much compensation. That New Year's Eve, a girl from school hosted a massive house party. I didn't go. I had already missed so many social events – what was one more? I had been in a hospital bed while my friends were sneaking drinks from their parents' booze cabinets and hoping the boys they fancied would kiss them at midnight. I didn't need to celebrate the new year, anyway. As far as I was concerned, I would never enjoy a year, or anything at all, again.

A few weeks on, the physical pain had begun to subside. I just had to face the mental turmoil. I was the only person I knew with one eye. Once I was fully healed, I would have to walk back into class with a part of me missing – a part I had loved.

I turned away from the mirror and gently put pressure on the underside of the socket, trying to dislodge the prosthesis from its cavity. In an unpractised and clumsy motion I managed to eject it, but wasn't quick enough to grab it with my left hand. The acrylic appendage slid forward and into the sink. I caught it as it started to circle the plughole and dropped it into the saline solution I had been given at the hospital. I didn't like sleeping with the eye in; it felt foreign and hard against my head.

I looked in the mirror again. What was left in its place was swollen and sore. I couldn't look into the fleshy void for long without needing to sit down. I couldn't believe that this was actually happening to me. I couldn't believe I had just popped my fake eye out and left it to soak for the night. I couldn't believe I could see what lay behind my eyeball, like I had been subjected to a gruesome death on the battlefield in a *Game of Thrones* episode. Everything I had feared the most had come true, and I was still coming to terms with that.

I stepped out of my slippers and climbed under the sheets of my mum's bed. I had slept there every night since my diagnosis. I didn't want to be alone, which worked well because she wanted me close, too. She hadn't come up to bed yet – I guessed she was probably downstairs watching telly. I didn't want to sit down there with her. I didn't want to talk. I didn't want to laugh or cry. I didn't even want comfort. No kind words could have convinced me that my life would ever be the same again.

I leant over and switched off the light. I pulled the duvet right up around my neck to shield me from the winter chill. I experienced the unfamiliar feeling of closing my eyes and having one set of lids connect over nothing but a gaping hole. *Why are you still closing that eye when the eyeball's been removed?* Every movement came with its own reminder.

I kept my eyes closed and willed myself to sleep. At least when I was asleep the pain took a break, and my mind didn't race. I was finally free for a few hours before I had to get up and face another day.

1

The beginning

If we're saying it how it is, Sarah has always been fit. She's got fresh, glowing skin from a lifetime of picking the right face creams, along with long hair that changes colour and style with the moving trends and her personal whims. It's the main perk of being a talented hair stylist, I suppose. When I look at photos of her from twenty-five years ago, it seems like very little has changed. Some people just end up with genes that make time stand still. Luckily for me she's my mum, so I'm hoping I inherited non-ageing DNA from her.

It's not just her looks, though. She's open, kind and positive, and always tries to see the best in people. She's been like that all my life. As you can imagine, a woman with attributes like that got a lot of attention from the fellas. She was twenty-five when she had me – these days I guess that would make her a young mum. But she already had my two older sisters Georgia (five) and Lauren (four).

Their dad, Gary, was her first love. In his younger years, Gary was a bit of a lad. He had always been popular with the women of Horsham, but he made a beeline for Mum. The two quickly became besotted with each other. But with the turbulence of young love, they struggled to make it stick. It was one of those relationships that blazed thick and fast, but combusted with the same amount of energy. When it was good, it was great. But when it broke down, it crashed and burned.

After one break-up, my mum started seeing Jason. Jason and Gary were part of the same group of blokes who hung out at the pub. From what I gather, they were both ladies' men in their own way. Mum and Jason spent a year locked in a fun flirtation that neither of them saw as a forever thing. I guess Mum needed a fling after the intensity of her long-term relationship with Gary, and enjoyed Jason's charms. But the low-commitment dating suddenly took a more serious turn when Mum found out she was pregnant. Even though it wasn't planned, it wasn't the earth-shattering moment some people experience when they discover an unexpected pregnancy. She already had two gorgeous daughters, so she was no stranger to motherhood, or to the work and routine required to raise children.

But for Jason, or Dad as I call him, this came as a huge shock. He didn't have any kids, so getting his head around the momentous change of becoming a father took time.

As we can all imagine, Gary wasn't impressed that his long-term ex and the mother of his children was having a baby with someone he knew well. It took time for tensions to soften, but Gary and Mum did give it one more shot after I was born. They were together for a couple of years.

My parents never made their relationship official, and weren't together when I was born, so we've never all lived in the same home. Some people have asked if I find this upsetting, being a child from a 'broken home'. But in reality, I can't think of anything worse than having Mum and Dad under the same roof. They're polar opposites, and I can imagine that us all living together would be a nightmare. They're happy with their situations. My mum is now with her husband John, whom she met about ten years ago. And my dad lives nearby, so I drop round to see him weekly for a catch-up and a cup of tea. This means I get to be close with them both. These days we all get on, including Gary and his wife, who join us for family events and parties, particularly when we're celebrating big days for Georgia and Lauren.

Good things come in threes

Rolling back twenty-seven years, Mum experienced the now-familiar nausea and took a pregnancy test. When two blue lines appeared, she knew she was about to do it all over again. At her twelve-week scan, the sonographer told her she had actually conceived twins, but that my counterpart had died in the womb. This is probably the least painful way to find out you've lost a child. Most people go into their scans expecting and hoping to have one healthy baby, and that's what she was told she would be having. It's hard to grieve a person you never knew existed, so the loss was reasonably easy for her to bear.

I remember being told that I was originally a twin when I was younger. I thought about it a lot. There are certain things that are a far bigger feature in your childhood than in your adulthood, like tractors and quicksand and yoghurt. I could add being a twin to that list. When Mum explained what had happened, I asked if I could name him. We assumed it was a little boy, although he wasn't sufficiently developed for us to know. Mum agreed that I could, so I allocated him the name Harry.

In time my memory faded, and I forgot that I had been the one to come up with the name. To my mind I'd always had a twin called Harry who passed away before I was born. I think naming him allowed me to process what I was being told. My twin stopped being just a mass of cells in my mind and became a person, which allowed me to acknowledge the loss. Even as a little child, I thought about what my life would have been like if he had been born. I loved my sisters, but there was an age gap between us, and when they went off to stay with Gary, I went to my dad's on my own. I often thought about what it would have been like to do that as a pair. But daydreams like that fade with age, and there are enough things in life to concern ourselves with. I haven't thought about my alternative Harry reality in years.

The pregnancy continued as expected. Mum's nausea gradually subsided and her belly grew. She would rest her hand on the top of her stomach as I kicked and elbowed myself around to find a comfortable position. Caring for two young children while pregnant isn't easy, but Gary had the girls every other weekend. Dad would drop in to make sure Mum was doing OK, and she also had her parents around to help.

Two weeks before I was born, Mum was walking through Horsham town centre when she fell over. She lost her footing on some uneven paving and, with the additional weight on her front, was thrown off balance and toppled over, face forwards, hitting her bump on the floor as she fell. Passers-by rushed over to help and see if she was OK. People can be in their own worlds at times, but I've found when it comes to pregnancy and small children, everyone feels a duty of care.

After fetching her some water and making sure she was steady on her feet, the crowd dispersed. Concerned for the baby inside her after such a nasty fall, Mum decided to go straight to the hospital. The doctors checked her over. They confirmed there was no damage and nothing to be concerned about. For the next fortnight, Mum tried to take it easy as she prepared for my arrival.

A shocking start

The evening before Mum gave birth, Nan and Grandad came over with a curry. Through the night, Mum could feel her stomach cramping and seizing up. Convinced she'd picked a curry with too much kick, she tried to ignore it and go back to sleep. In the morning the pains intensified, so she called Nan, who came round to help. Nan took one look at her and called an ambulance. There was no point taking any risks when she was clearly in so much pain, and with a full-term baby due any day.

The paramedics came and spent some time examining Mum. They asked a series of questions, and prodded and poked in the way that medical professionals do best. Eventually, they decided it was safest to take her to the hospital for a full check-up. You can never be too careful when it comes to pregnancy.

She was lying on the gurney with Nan sitting on the fold-down seat next to her, and that's when her waters broke. To everyone's dismay, the fluid was murky and brown. They immediately knew that something was wrong. Mum was rushed straight to the delivery ward, where she was handed over to the midwives.

What the doctors hadn't realised was that the fall had dislodged the umbilical cord, so I hadn't received any food or nutrients from my mum for fourteen days. I had been starved and wasn't well at all.

I came out less than an hour after the ambulance ride. I was born blue, like I'd been left in the freezer. I was so undernourished that waiting for Mum's milk to come in and for me to latch onto the breast wasn't an option. They handed me straight to my auntie Amanda, who fed me from a bottle. She was the first person to hold me.

The staff at the hospital had a job on their hands to restore me and Mum to full health after such a difficult birth. Mum was poorly for days after, and I needed round-the-clock care to make sure I was feeding regularly and growing in strength. Thankfully, my lifelong love of food kicked in early, and it wasn't long before I was a healthy weight and colour. My cheeks filled out and I no longer looked like a sickly baby but a thriving chunk, ready to demand attention and to put anything and everything in my mouth.

These days, we would expect the father to be in the delivery room with the mother, but back in the 90s that wasn't always the case. My dad left my nan and auntie to stay with Mum during the birth. But once I was born and had received some initial emergency care, he was in there like a shot, holding me and placing a gigantic finger in my tiny palm to see if I would grasp hold of him. He was so chuffed.

My sisters were still young when I was born. When I asked them what they remembered of my birth, it was little to nothing. We have photos from the first day I came home from the hospital. The two of them were sitting on the sofa, and I had been carefully positioned on their laps, with my dad at the back. No doubt my nan was just out of shot, poised to dive in and grab me if they made any sudden moves.

2
Happy families

Life at home was busy. It was one of those houses that was never quiet. Peace had to be found among the chaos of three young girls.

Meet the grandparents

My dad is one of six, but I never met his parents, Monty and Anne, because they died before I was born. I've always called them Nanny Anne and Grandad Monty, as they weren't able to pick nicknames for themselves. They both passed away far younger than they should have, but I know they were family-oriented, much like me and the rest of our family.

When you don't get to meet people in person, you build a picture of them in your head – like when you read about a character in a book, or before you meet up with someone you've matched with on a dating app. I've had to allow my imagination to fill the gaps in the stories I've been told about their characters and lives.

I know Grandad Monty was well loved. I've pictured myself jumping onto his lap and him pretending to have stolen my nose. I know from Dad that Nanny Anne had some personal issues she struggled with, but I feel sure she would have been fiercely protective of me, and shown me the most love and affection. There would probably have been Werther's Originals around. I reckon they would have snuck me sweets and then said they had no idea why I was so hyper.

I saw a lot of Dad's brothers and sisters growing up though, along with their children, my cousins. As I was his only child, it was nice that he could take me to hang out with them from time to time. We visited Uncle Tyrone in Cornwall and Uncle Martin in Devon for beach holidays. I also hung out with Uncle Dominic, Auntie Sally and Auntie Sandra a lot, as they lived closer by. Uncle Dominic's daughter, Annie-Rose, was around my age. We watched movies together and begged our parents to let us have sleepovers.

In a bizarre twist that felt a bit like something out of a movie, we found out four years ago that Dad has a half-sister, Christine. Our family had always known Christine, but she never knew who her father was. She was friends with my aunties, Sally and Sandra, and people always said they looked alike. After years of speculation about whether or not they were related, Sandra gave Christine a hair sample and saliva swab for a DNA test. It came back as a match! Her father was Grandad Monty. I'm not here to judge, but probably the less I say about the circumstances the better!

The discovery was bittersweet, because it was too late for her to build a relationship with her biological dad. But suddenly I had a new auntie, and she had six brothers and sisters. She was already close with our family, but now she was really part of it. I love spending time with her, and she's become an important part of my life.

I wasn't short of people to love me on my mum's side either. Mum is one of three. She has a brother, Chris, and a sister, Mandy, so we had aunties, uncles and cousins coming out of our ears and we loved every one of them. Plus, Nan and Grandad – mum's parents, Margaret and Ronald – lived three roads away, so we were constantly at theirs or they at ours. We were inseparable.

When Mum went back to her full-time job at the hairdresser's, they took on the bulk of the childcare. Nan is seventy-three but, much like Mum, you wouldn't know it. People often ask if she's my mum because of those age-defying genes. She's still got the same blonde, mid-length hair I remember from when I was a child. She takes time over her appearance, straightening her locks and applying a dab of make-up to her face every morning.

Nan's signature style is a maxi skirt, although they were just called long skirts when she started wearing them. As a very young child I would grab the flowing material around her ankles as I played, to indicate that she should either crouch down to play with me or pick me up so I could join her way up there. She's always decked out in bright colours and big, glam jewellery. She's witty, with a sharp sense of humour; not so sharp that you'd cut yourself, but sharp enough that it took some time to get used to. The best advice I can give is that if you don't want someone to ask your boyfriend an embarrassing question, don't introduce him to my nan. But on the plus side, if you want an answer to a question you don't feel you can ask, she's your ideal wingwoman. So it's swings and roundabouts, really.

My nan also taught me about spirituality. She's been a Christian her whole life. She prayed for us and explained all about her beliefs as I grew up, so I get my faith in God from her. Tracking through the story of my life, I've been certain there are things that can't have happened by accident. Some things are just too coincidental to be coincidence.

Nan always made sure that everyone who came to the house knew about her faith and got the standard quiz about their own. You can imagine how much three teenage girls loved that when we all started dating! She is, and was, unapologetically herself. When she doesn't agree with a decision, she continues to be supportive and loving, even if she ends up having to help pick up the pieces afterwards. She's not an 'I told you so' type person, but is filled with warmth and kindness.

As I got older, I would fold myself onto her lap, curling in as close as I could. She would stroke my hair and snuggle me in even tighter. What I remember most clearly from my childhood is her and my grandad's warmth. When I stayed at their house, I'd either sleep in their bed with them or they would make up a little bed for me right next to theirs. Grandad would let me pick one of his big T-shirts, which became my nightie.

Life with Mum

I was a year old when Mum, Georgia, Lauren and I moved from our two-bedroom house to a new home a couple of roads over. That's the house my mum still lives in today. We've always lived in

Horsham, and I can't ever see that changing. When all your family is so close, it would mean giving up a lot to leave. The area wasn't new to us, but we suddenly had more space. There were three bedrooms and a bigger lounge for us to play in.

At Mum's house, there was always food on the table. The house was always clean and tidy. We always got lovely Christmas and birthday presents, but money was tight. She had to work hard to make ends meet, and to save up to buy us the things we needed and the things we wanted. She made a lot of sacrifices for her daughters.

I loved being around my sisters back at Mum's house, but if I'm honest I don't think they loved being around me. With the five-year age gap, they found me annoying. I always wanted to play with them and fought hard for their attention, but what eight-year-old wants to stop what they're doing to watch CBeebies with their three-year-old sister? As we got older and the age gap narrowed, we got closer and closer, but as a young child I felt lonely at times. I responded to my feelings of rejection by playing up. Sometimes I got upset, other times I got angry. I would be naughty and then adamantly announce that it was Lauren or Georgia's fault, and nothing to do with me. Sometimes I would have a tantrum so persistent that Mum would call Dad. He would drive over to pick me up, take me out for a walk and help me to calm down.

There was one trip where Mum, Nan and Grandad took the three of us on holiday to Tunisia. While we were out there, Mum bought me a traditional Tunisian dress. It was red with a big puffy skirt and was covered in gold bells that jangled every time I moved. I vividly remember spinning around on the dancefloor in my new outfit, enjoying the racket the embellishments created.

Another less cheerful memory I have involved a trip to the local swimming pool. There were a couple of swimming pools at our council-run leisure centre. I was about three at the time, so I was placed in the baby pool with Georgia, who was seven. Bored of playing in a foot of water that didn't rise above her waist, Georgia decided to explore the big pool instead. I say big... Any adult could have comfortably stood in it without getting their shoulders wet, but for a child it was the real deal. Mum and Nan had taken Lauren out of the water and were sitting by the side of the pool, for reasons that are now lost in time.

My baby pool experience was cut short when Georgia decided the most sensible thing to do would be to take my pink rubber ring with her as a buoyancy aid for her adventures in the deep. Keen to continue playing with both my sister and the inflatable, I promptly got up and followed her over to the big pool. Having briefly taken their eyes off me, Mum and Nan realised I wasn't in the baby pool any more. They searched every face they could see and then Mum ran through the changing rooms, looking under doors and shouting through the showers to see if anyone had seen me. Nan sat by the side of the pool with Lauren, and started praying that I would appear, unharmed, that very minute.

But I wasn't there because I still had my eyes on the big pool prize. I jumped in, hoping to catch up with Georgia, only to feel myself sinking under the water. I couldn't swim. I wasn't even close to being able to doggy paddle. My flapping arms splashed my face, my mouth taking in gasp after gasp of pool water. Then I was submerged. I can't say for sure, but what I think I felt was a momentary sense of peace. I wasn't trying to get to the surface any more. I couldn't breathe, but I wasn't trying to.

All of a sudden, a hand gripped my small, chubby arm, and yanked. I was ripped from the brief underwater calm into a frantic crowd of onlookers. A lady had pulled me out of the water and sat me on the side, tapping my back to make sure any liquid I had inhaled came back up. The lifeguard bundled over to make sure I didn't need CPR. He cleared some space so I could catch my breath, then took me, hysterically crying, to find my mum and nan. We were reunited in a flurry of tears. Georgia, who may actually kill me for including this story, has felt guilty about it ever since. But thankfully, no harm was done in the end.

Life with Dad

I went to stay with Dad every other weekend. Splitting your time between two homes takes its toll – anyone whose parents are separated but still in their lives will tell you that. At this time, Dad was living in a caravan at a local motorhome park in Southwater, a small village outside Horsham. It had rolling hills, fields with sheep and a swimming lake that got packed on hot summer days. When I was there, it felt like I wasn't in the town any more, but very much in the countryside.

The site was a safe place for children to play, and they often hosted charity events and family fun days in the grounds. There was a clubhouse where we would go and have dinner, and it even had a little arcade where I could spend the fifty pence worth of two pence pieces Dad gave me on the coin pusher machine.

Dad got me a little electric scooter, and I remember whizzing around the caravan park at what felt like a Lewis Hamilton-like pace. There weren't many other families with kids around, but there was another little girl called Elise. We got on well and became firm friends. Every time I was there, I would ask Dad if I could run over to her caravan and knock for her, and then we would play out together. On a few occasions, Elise came into town with me, and we had a sleepover at Nan and Grandad's.

With the lack of other children around, Dad was always open to me bringing my friends down to the caravan park for the weekend. He was always very generous with me. It took him a while to catch up with banking technology, so for a long time he carried his money around in cash. He wouldn't buy me absolutely anything I asked for, but I knew that I could get away with asking for more from Dad than from Mum.

While Mum's budget had to stretch to the three of us, I was Dad's only child, so I took every opportunity I got to go down to the shops with him. A lot of the stuff we did together would be things grown-ups did, rather than activities geared towards children. We'd go and see his mates, run a few errands or pop into the pub. Most of the time I didn't really feel as if I could chip into the grown-up conversations. He often took me to the cinema though, which I loved. We would see whatever kids' film was out that week, and he would buy me a Tango Ice Blast and a big bucket of sugar popcorn.

3

A class act

I didn't enjoy every stage of my education, but when it came to nursery, I had a great time. My memories of those early years' reading times and sticky collage are priceless to me. I started nursery at the age of three, and it was there that I met Elisha. Elisha was loud and fun and took everything in her stride. We became inseparable and, luckily for us, it was her nan who ran the place, so we had friends in high places.

Elisha often came over to my nan's house after preschool, and we would have tea and keep the games going for a few extra hours. Elisha's two older sisters were the same ages as mine, so the six of us got on well. Elisha and I were quickly joined by my cousin Megan, and our energetic trio was branded 'the Three Musketeers'.

After nursery, the three of us moved on to a school in Little Haven, and I'm pleased to say that the roots we put down as we skipped over stepping stones in the playground served us well, as we're still friends today. Don't get me wrong, there were fallouts from time to time – usually over boys – but we always got over them quickly. Well... not that quickly, because we still joke about some of the adolescent man-stealing that went on.

The most serious argument we had came when I stole some penny sweets from the local shop. Bad, I know, but I was in my naughty kid phase and decided the best way to act out was to pocket the treats and take them to school with me. We were in primary school at the time, and I confided in Elisha and Megan that I had committed the crime. Shortly afterwards, I saw Elisha talking to a teacher in the playground and was convinced that my bestie had turned informant. I ran into the cloakroom, and both Megan and Elisha came running in after me. I was furious, and we started shouting at each other. The arguing turned into actual fighting, and I threw my lunchbox at Elisha. It wasn't my finest moment, and she ended up with a big scratch down her face.

After the shock of the 'attack by meal deal' had subsided, we snapped out of it and hugged, and I apologised. That wasn't the end of it though, as the teachers noticed the mark on Elisha's face. We were marched to the head teacher's office to explain what had happened. I was suspended for a day for scratching Elisha's face, then everything returned to normal.

Dancing and romancing

Every term finished in true 00s style with a disco. As the years went on and we became some of the oldest in primary school, the hype around these events escalated. We all wanted to look our best for an afternoon of standing across the room from all the boys. Luckily for me, my mum was a hairdresser, so she would give me a salon-worthy hairstyle for each event. I opted for a ponytail with stiff spikes poking out. Mum would send me on my way with my Spice Girls-esque hairstyle and a pound to buy sweets from the tuck shop.

At the dance we would play a game where the boys and girls faced opposite walls and then backed towards each other into the middle of the room. Whoever you bumped into you had to slow dance with. I would always try to line up with Glen – it was silly to leave these things to chance. A cheeky lad, he was good at football and always had his hair in spikes. Sadly, loads of other girls fancied Glen and had the same idea, so there would be a cluster standing directly opposite him. This meant that the chances of reversing into romance with Glen were low.

I did eventually manage to pin my man down and, for a brief period at the age of ten, the most popular guy in school was my boyfriend. My sisters were well aware of my crush, as I was outed by social media network Bebo. Glen created a little montage where his profile picture faded into my profile picture, accompanied by one of my favourite songs. That's when we went public with our love. After that, all bets were off.

I remember him posting on my page: 'I will love you until there are no stars left in the sky.' To which I replied: 'I love you more than my Nintendo Wii.' But despite such grand declarations, we kept our romance very low-key. Kissing happened, but it was only ever on the cheek and usually followed by a lot of giggling.

We once went on a date to the cinema. Mum and her boyfriend came too, but we went to see different films. Glenn and I watched *The Water Horse*, a kids' film about the Loch Ness Monster.

Sadly, it didn't last. We broke up in the summer between primary and secondary school, and I thought my little heart would never heal from the pain.

Home and away

Despite the tricky ending, I had a good group of friends at primary school, and I enjoyed it. Mum always cut my hair into a short bob. I wanted to look as girly as possible, so I hated it. I was always jealous of the girls with long, flowing locks. I was also sporting a monobrow that I hadn't yet thought to pluck. But I loved my eyes. My deep chestnut eyes were my favourite thing about my face.

Most of the time I was well behaved. I had my moments, like anyone, but on the whole I wasn't one of the kids who messed around and disrupted the class.

It was at home that I was struggling. My mum's boyfriend at the time was a difficult person to be around. He was controlling and didn't treat her well. He was also prone to fits of anger, so I was always on edge when he was around. I struggled to sleep and some-times had nightmares. I usually climbed out of bed and snuggled in next to my mum, but if he was staying I couldn't, so I would just cry out for her instead. On one occasion he made it very clear that he was not willing to put up with that.

He sought help for his rage issues, but insisted that Mum and I also attend anger management sessions. It felt like he was trying to shift the blame on to us. My mum relented, so I had a child therapist come and speak to me in school about how to respond in different upsetting scenarios. Thankfully, they had broken up by the time I went to secondary school.

Big Nanny and Great-Grandad

It wasn't just my nan I had a close relationship with. I was also lucky enough to get to meet my great-nan and great-grandad – Nan's parents. It was around this time, when I was eleven years old, that my great-nan passed away. She and my great-grandad lived a five-minute walk from our house, and they had a massive garden.

I used to call her 'Big Nanny', but that didn't go down well. Every time I said it, she would correct me. She was devoted to her Catholic faith, which brought her a lot of hope, but because of her age and the strict religious environment she had been raised in, she came across as a little stern to me.

When I got older, I was told that she'd faced great hardships in her life, suffering abuse at the hands of a family member and being forced by alcoholic parents to step up and look after her younger siblings. Perhaps that's why she was so serious.

My great-grandad had a warmer demeanour. We got on so well. He would take me into the garden to show me his vegetable patch and his beehive. Great-grandad was born and raised in Poland, where he lived until it was invaded in 1939, during the Second World War. His story was like something out of a movie. I'm sad that he never wrote a book, as it would have been a gripping tale of kidnap, battles and eventually driving a tank for the Americans. After the war he couldn't go back to his home in Poland, so he moved to the UK and ultimately settled in Horsham, where he met my great-nan and rescued her from her horrific living conditions. My great-nan wrote an autobiography before she died, and in it she credited my great-grandad for saving her from all the pain of her young life. He never stopped being a hero. He was always determined, independent and, most importantly, kind. They were completely in love.

When I was little, they would hand me the biscuit tin when we visited and let me pick my favourite. She would ask how I was, and

15

I would get shy and curl up on my mum's lap, letting her answer for me. I wasn't old enough to know that it was important to push through the discomfort to get to know someone. They had an old-fashioned marbles game where you had to make the marbles jump over each other to clear the board. I busied myself with it for hours.

I was ten when we found out Great-nan had cancer. She'd already had a few scares, and had survived blood cancer, but my nan sat me down one day and explained that Great-nan had been diagnosed with blood cancer. I was young and didn't fully understand what was going on, but it became clear that Great-nan was very unwell as she became increasingly frail and poorly. She didn't want to talk about the cancer when we went round, so the visits became even more upsetting.

My nan looked after her in her last days. She was adamant that she wanted to stay at home and refused to go into a care home. A year after receiving her diagnosis she passed away.

This was my first introduction to the concept of death. We went to their house to pay our respects, and she was still lying in her bed. My mum didn't think it was appropriate for me to see her body at rest, but I was desperate to be like all the adults and say my goodbye properly. She decided to let me.

As I approached the bed, I realised I'd made a mistake. She didn't look like the stern, strong woman I had known. She was pale and had lost her hair. Her eyes were still open, and she looked gaunt from the weight she'd lost during her treatment. I felt scared.

From then on, it felt like there was a dark shadow hanging over their house. When I went to visit Great-grandad I preferred to stay outdoors, walking around the garden or playing on the lawn. I was sad to have lost Great-nan and glad to have known her, as so many people don't know anyone from that generation of their family. But what I remember most was a completely new feeling.

I was terrified of dying.

4

Pre-teen dream

Starting secondary school opened my world up just a bit wider. I felt as if I was stepping into adulthood. I'd seen my sisters get ready and go off to secondary for years, carrying loads of books and rolling up their skirt waistbands. I wanted to be just like them. By the time I joined, Georgia was in her final year and Lauren was in the year below her, so I got to see them to begin with. Mum took me round a few schools, but in the end we opted for Millais School, a girls' school in Horsham, mainly because I wanted to be like my sisters.

The school was strict, but plenty of people wanted to go there because the pupils got good grades. They were militant about making sure our checked skirts reached to our knees, and that our shirts were properly tucked in. We did our best to push back, customising the clothes as best we could without getting told off.

Many people would have been worried about going to a single-sex school, but for me it was just right. The Forest School for boys was next door, so we would meet up with the boys at home time and often walk back together. I found that more exciting than sitting in classes with them all day. We would gossip and giggle about who we fancied, and then we got the chance to catch a glimpse of them after school.

I enjoyed the logic of maths and science and was good at those at first, although my interest in these subjects waned as I got older. The humanities held less appeal to me. I couldn't get on board with geography and, despite holding to the faith introduced to me by my nan, I didn't enjoy religious studies either. I think it was because there was so much writing, and I found my attention trailed off easily. PE was always a fun subject, as it meant we got to run around. I enjoyed the break from the monotony of the classroom. That doesn't mean I was any good at sports, because I wasn't. But it's the taking part that counts, right?

The social scene

Megan and Elisha were also at Millais, so the Three Musketeers continued their adventures. The dynamics changed slightly, though. Megan was in my form group, so we spent a lot of time together, but Elisha was in a different class and formed tight friendships with the girls around her.

As well as spending time with Megan, I made a new group of friends. We formed a little gaggle, and would eat together at lunch, go to each other's houses and hang out after school. Dana was the coolest girl of the gang and all the boys seemed to fancy her.

As my mum was a bit younger than most of the others, she was always very relaxed about me going out and having friends round. People used to love coming over to mine, and Mum would give us snacks and let us play loud music. We would head into town to meet up with the lads. I was still feeling stung by the dramatic Glen break-up, but I managed to put it behind me when I met Oli.

Oli looked like he should be in a boy band. When we first met, his dark-brown hair was spiked up, but sometimes he'd have a moody fringe brushed to the sides and other times he'd shave it off completely. Like his hair, his clothes changed with the preferred get-up of the day. At this point we were all wearing McKenzie tracksuits, but later we ventured into the emo world of dark colours and wide-leg jeans.

I wasn't the only one who liked Oli. Whenever he was around, I felt so nervous that I wouldn't be able to say a word. It was during one of these hangouts in town when my vow of embarrassed silence was broken by a new girl called Lou.

With some people you meet you have to work hard to think of what to say next and you're desperate for the day when you just know each other well enough that there is no awkwardness, just fun. That wasn't Lou. From the instant we met, we couldn't stop talking. It was like we were two magnets pulling together. I felt good about myself when I was around her, like I was fun and interesting.

We quickly became inseparable, caught up in one of those all-consuming friendships that you only have time for when you're at school. Lou had a rebellious streak; she talked back to people and often got into trouble. I admired her fiery spirit. She was surrounded by friends, but always made a beeline for me.

Lou went to a mixed school called Tanbridge House on the other side of town, and in a fit of enthusiasm for our friendship, I begged my mum to let me change schools to be with her. I don't know if it was my powers of persuasion or if Mum preferred the other one anyway, but she agreed to the transfer.

It was halfway through year seven that I moved to Tanbridge. Initially, I was given a trial to see if I liked the school, and if I would perform well enough academically to stick around.

It was very different going to a mixed school, and my behaviour took a swift downturn. Lou's rejection of authority began to rub off on me, and within weeks we were skipping lessons to run down to Tesco to buy lunch. When we were in a class together our only focus was on messing around and having fun. Our poor music teacher didn't stand a chance with us sitting next to each other, surrounded by instruments.

Acts of truancy and misbehaviour meant I didn't pass the probation period, so I was booted out and sent back to Millais. Mum was furious that I had got into so much trouble that they wouldn't have me, and I was banned from spending time with Lou. With all the adults involved agreeing that we were no good together, we were kept apart. We occasionally managed to sneak away to meet up, but the difficulty of clandestine meet-ups quickly became too much, and we abandoned all hope of hanging out together.

Despite having my Italian exercise book covered in Oli's name, I did have other flirtations and even kisses in that first year of secondary school. My first kiss happened when I was twelve, with a boy called Sebastian. He was from the same town, and even to this day I bump into him at the supermarket sometimes. A group of us were hanging out in the Youth Wing – a space where kids from Millais and Forest gathered on a Friday after school. We were messing around and playing games, and suddenly my friends all pushed me towards him and chanted to make us kiss.

This wasn't just the Glen kind of cheek kiss; it was full on tongue action. I couldn't tell you if it was a good kiss or nor, it all went by in a whirlwind. But I do remember that I had no idea what I was doing. As he leaned in, I committed the cardinal sin of keeping my eyes open. To be fair, I'd had no training, so how was I supposed to know that it was best to keep them shut? One of the guys shouted out: 'What? Liv! Have you got your eyes open?' Everyone laughed, and I was so embarrassed that I messaged my mum to come and pick me up early.

It was an eventful year, full of all the things pre-teens do when they're trying to work out how to move into adulthood. I felt I had everything ahead of me. Little did I know that it would be my last chance to mess about with my friends for a long time.

5

Teen nightmare

Having older sisters is the best and the worst. I loved them and wanted to be just like them. But as I've already explained, they sometimes found me annoying.

I often felt protected by my older sisters. It helped that they were so popular at school. They were both pretty with long, flowing blonde hair. They wore jewellery and make-up, and dressed like the girls in *More* magazine. They had a few boyfriends when they were teenagers, and I remember that one of Lauren's could beatbox. I was amazed by him, and would ask him to perform every time he came round.

I was twelve when Lauren got glasses. She was eighteen and didn't need to wear them all the time, just when she was reading and looking at things close up. While most people would prefer not to have glasses, I was convinced that I needed them myself. I wanted to be just like Lauren. I begged my mum to take me to Specsavers to have an eye test, even fibbing that when I looked at things close up, they were a little blurry. Once again, I managed to nag my mum into submission, and she booked me in for an eye test.

Mum had to work that day, so it was Nan who came into town with me. I was hopeful that I could persuade her and the optician that I needed a prescription. I sat in the chair and called out the letters on the screen positioned on the other side of the room. I did the red and green light test, covering each eye to see if it made a difference. It's a routine that anyone with glasses is used to, but it was my first time.

The black mist

Next the optician asked me to position my chin on a plastic chin rest so she could look inside my eye. I held still while she performed her examination. I wasn't sure what was normal, but it felt like I was having to hold still for a long time. She rolled some sort of device from left to right, then back again, scanning my eye, which started to feel dry as I strained to hold it open. Then she got up quite abruptly and said she wanted to speak to another optician. She told me I had an unusual black mist in my eye that someone else would need to take a look at. She left the room, and I was relieved to finally be able to blink and sit comfortably in my chair.

She came back a moment later with another optician. I had to get back into position with the uncomfortable chin rest and then he performed the same ritual, looking up and down, left and right around my eye.

Afterwards, the man sat back in his seat. I did the same, once again enjoying the release.

He said: 'I can see the same black mist my colleague reported. Usually when I see something like this, it's a cataract. But given that you're so young, that would be extremely rare. I'd like you to go to Horsham Hospital, just so they can check you over and confirm.'

He didn't seem particularly worried or panicked, and neither were we. Nan just said that it was strange, and I would have to come out of school for a half-day to go to the hospital appointment. I was secretly delighted that I would get to skip a few lessons for an eye test. I thought I might even come home with some sweet new glasses, just like Lauren's.

A week later my mum took me to the hospital, where a doctor used the same machine to look deep into my eye. He said he thought I had a cataract but, once again, he was confused as to how, at the age of twelve, I could have this. He continued to run tests and ask me questions, and was particularly interested when I said that I had a black floater in my right eye that moved around with my vision. I'd had this slightly darker patch in my sight for years but hadn't thought anything of it. I assumed that's what everyone saw, as I didn't know any different. The doctor decided that this was sufficiently unusual to warrant additional tests, so this time he asked me to travel down to Brighton General Hospital, where they had a bigger ophthalmology department and more advanced equipment.

Two weeks later, Nan drove me and Mum to Brighton for yet another eye test. The routine was becoming pretty familiar by this point, and when the specialist had finished poking around he confirmed he had also seen the black mist in my eye. But he said he was certain it wasn't a cataract. He couldn't say for sure what it was, but he was able to rule out this theory, so at least that was something.

After a lengthy examination and consultation, he pulled Mum to one side. He told her he was going to refer me to St Bartholomew's Hospital in London, and that he needed us to go the following day. He said the referral would be to the oncology ward – where they treated cancer patients – but that she shouldn't worry. He said that was just where they were able to do the best exploratory work with eyes.

Despite his reassurances, Mum was suddenly very concerned. It hadn't occurred to any of us that this was very serious, but the situation had escalated. She told my nan what he had said, and between them they agreed that they wouldn't mention anything about oncology or cancer. I was only twelve, and there was no need to worry me unnecessarily.

A trip to London

The next day was a Friday, so I took another day off school for the follow-up appointment. Mum and Nan barely slept, and spent the whole train journey to London running through worst-case scenarios in their heads. I was oblivious. I had just secured a second day off when I wasn't even ill, plus I was getting a day trip to London. I also had a ticket to a regular under-18s club night that evening, so I would be heading to Liquid Envy to dance with my friends, and hopefully Oli would be there. As far as I was concerned, things were looking good.

We got off at London Victoria and just had time to grab some food from the M&S Simply Food shop at the station that we would eat later for lunch. I went for my favourite small pot of pesto pasta, while Mum had a couscous salad and Nan had her usual duck wrap.

When we got to the hospital, I was ushered straight in for a series of scans and to undergo a few tests. Then we sat in the waiting room to eat our meal deals while we waited for news from the doctor. The consultant, whose name was Mr Hungerford, swung open the door and poked his head out. 'Olivia Deane?'

All three of us bundled into the room behind him, along with two nurses who followed us in. It was dark. The lights had been turned down low and there was a lightbox mounted on the wall with a scan on it. We took our seats on the visitor side of his desk, and he didn't allow a moment's pause before he started talking: 'I'm really sorry to inform you, but you have a form of cancer called retinoblastoma in your right eye.'

And that's when my world ended.

I'm sure he carried on talking, but I couldn't tell you what he said after that. My head started swimming. I had so many questions that I needed the answers to all at once. Only there was a bottleneck in my brain, and I couldn't get anything to come out of my mouth. I sat there, completely still, my eyes fixed on him, watching his mouth move as he continued to explain. It was a slow-motion tidal wave crashing through my head, drowning out my thoughts and my consciousness.

Suddenly the world felt heavy. A day off school wasn't important any more, and neither was an under-18s club night.

I had cancer.

Am I going to die?

Those are the words we all dread needing to ask. The thing we hope won't ever happen to us. I thought about the adverts I had seen on TV asking people to donate to cancer charities. I thought about the people they showed in extreme pain, with no hair and tubes attached to their bodies. I thought back to my great-nan, the only person I knew who'd had cancer. I thought of her frailty and the fact that she had died.

I was going to die. That was what people with cancer did. They died.

I wanted to ask about this, to clarify whether I had just heard an announcement about my own death, but I was too embarrassed. I thought he might think it was a silly question, so I just kept staring at him.

My mum was standing behind me. She leant forwards and put her hand on my shoulder as I tried to swallow the news. It was nice to feel something. I put my hand on hers, pressing it with my fingers, confirming in this small gesture that I wasn't alone.

I was diseased. I was ill. I was going to be the sick girl. I couldn't imagine telling my schoolfriends that I had cancer. And definitely not the boys. I pictured myself losing my hair – the hair I had always moaned about having in a bob, that I had dreamed of growing out like Lauren and Georgia. But what was the point now? It was all going to drop out and I would be a bald twelve-year-old. Everyone would laugh at me. Or worse, pity me.

I turned to look at Mum and saw there were tears streaming down her face. I could hear her frantically trying to catch her breath as she sobbed. A nurse was hugging her, trying to offer some comfort. Nan was also crying.

I wanted to, but again I felt embarrassed. The idea of crying made me feel self-conscious. I was at the centre of this devastation, and I wanted it to end. I wanted to airlift myself out of there and back to my maths class at Millais, where I could mess about with Megan and talk about Oli.

My thought process was interrupted when Mr Hungerford said: 'Do you have any questions?'

Yes, I had every question. Questions were the only thing I had in that moment. And yet still nothing came out. He waited patiently, giving me the space to order my thoughts.

Eventually, I spluttered out: 'Am I going to die?'

He met my gaze with a warm, reassuring expression. 'The worst-case scenario would be that you lose your eye, but we're going to do our best to stop that from happening.'

I suppose with his expertise he knew the most likely outcomes, and death wasn't one of them. But as with any form of cancer, it wasn't completely impossible.

After the initial dust had settled, Mr Hungerford talked us through the various treatment options for retinoblastoma. He explained the process of chemotherapy and the different types available. He explained that it would shrink the tumour in the eye and hopefully completely eradicate it without the need for surgery. His firm, unshaking voice gave me the reassurance I needed. I made the decision there and then to be hopeful. He was hopeful, so I would be too. I refused to even entertain the idea that I would lose my eye. It was just not going to happen.

He explained that it was very rare for anyone over the age of five to be diagnosed with a retinoblastoma. I was the first person he'd ever seen of my age, but he had previously treated a seven-year-old with the same condition. They didn't know if I'd had the tumour since I was a baby and it had grown very slowly up until this point, or if it was something that had just come on.

The final blow in this barrage of life-changing information was that the tumour was growing quickly, so they wanted me to have my first round of chemotherapy in just two weeks' time. As he continued to explain what that would mean for me, my body and my life, the realities of the road ahead started to become apparent.

I might lose my hair. I might feel awful, and be unable to move or function properly. I might feel so sick that I wouldn't be able to eat. I would have to miss school. I would miss time with my friends. I wouldn't be able to run about with everyone, hanging out at the Youth Wing kissing boys or ditching geography lessons to get lunch at Tesco. My life was about to completely change.

There was so much to absorb that Mr Hungerford suggested I take a breather. They had a playroom available for children to amuse themselves in while the doctors chatted to the parents. I was too old for the toys and mats, but I did need the break.

I went in and sat down with the nurses, Laura and Dawn, who were 'play specialists'. They were there to look after the young patients. They were gentle and kind, but also fun and encouraging. They didn't patronise me, but they showed me care and affection. I felt at home with them straight away.

They explained that I would go over to Great Ormond Street Hospital for the chemo, but that they would be there every time I came in, to sit with me and chat to me. I felt so grateful when I heard that.

I tried to ask them questions and they guided me a bit, but said it was best to wait and talk it all through with the doctors at Great Ormond Street when I went in for my appointment. They reassured me that these doctors had studied conditions like mine their whole lives. They told me about Dr Kingston, the incredible woman who would be part of my treatment, and who had made it her life's work to help people recover from cancer.

Before we left the hospital, they also checked Mum and Nan's eyes to make sure that the condition wasn't genetic. Thankfully it wasn't – we had enough to deal with as it was. At least there was some good news that day.

I sat in silence on the train ride home. I couldn't understand why this was happening to me. It wasn't happening to anyone else; it was happening to me. I was with Mum and Nan, but despite their best attempts at comforting me, I felt so alone. I wanted to feel normal. I was desperate to feel the way I had that morning, when I was just an average girl trying to figure out what to wear to the party that night.

When I got home, I went straight up to my room and started putting on my dress for the club. My mum stood in the doorway and said: 'You don't still want to go to Liquid tonight, do you?'

But I did. It sounds crazy when I think about it now, but I had two weeks left before the first course of chemotherapy started, and we had no idea how it would affect me. I wanted to be normal, to talk about boys and to see if anyone managed to get a snog that night.

'Yes, Mum,' I said. 'I really want to go and see my friends.'

She was concerned. It hadn't occurred to her that I would still consider going after the day we'd had. 'You've been through a lot today, Liv,' she said. 'I think you should stay at home and relax. It will take a while for all of this to sink in.'

But I insisted. Staying home wasn't going to change what had happened. It wouldn't make the road ahead any easier. Even though I still hadn't worked out what to make of it all, I knew I wanted to let my hair down. I wanted to be young, to be around people whose problems were teenager-sized, not these horrific, serious, adult problems I had spent the day engulfed in.

I didn't know if I was OK, but I knew that I had to keep going. Getting on with life would become a vital part of my healing process. And sadly, I was about to face a lot of things I would need to heal from.

6

Growing pains

At the age of twelve, there was a lot I didn't understand about cancer. I felt like I was diseased, like I had done something to bring this on myself. I felt ashamed of the seriousness of the situation and didn't want to bring such a downer into my friendship group. To me, whatever was going on in my body was gross. Cancer was something that happened to weak people, so I must be weak. I didn't want people to look at me and see a sick person. I wanted them to see Liv, the fun-loving girl who danced to music and did her friends' hair.

The teens are a time when everyone is getting used to their own body and not always feeling completely at ease inside it. I had started my periods a few months before this. Just as I felt I was stepping into adulthood, I'd been swiped back again. I wouldn't be able to grow or become the woman I had planned to be. I thought of Dana and Megan, the way they laughed and ran about, and how all the boys fancied them. They were happy and healthy. I was ill, and in no time at all, that illness would take over my whole life. I just wanted to be normal.

But normal would have to change for me.

Sharing my news

I went to that club night. I put on a tight black-and-purple flowery bodycon skirt, a black vest top and a gold gypsy belt. It was all the rage at the time.

I can't remember much about the night, which I suppose isn't all that surprising. But it was there, at Liquid Envy under-18s, that I told the first person I had cancer. Her name was Harriet, and she was one of my friends from school.

We were inside the packed club – the kind that looks awful if you ever see it in the daylight without all the people – and we were standing to one side of the dancefloor when we got chatting. There was no alcohol at the party, but that didn't stop the gaggle of pre-teens from jumping around on the dancefloor. The whole room was high on life. Music boomed through the speakers, making the conversation more like a shouting match than a chat between friends.

'I've been to the hospital today,' I told her.

Some of my friends knew there was something wrong with my eye, and more had picked up on it when I wasn't at school, but no one expected it to be anything serious.

She looked surprised and sympathetic all at once. 'Oh no! What for?'

I took a big gulp of breath, having decided to tell her. I had to start somewhere, and with someone, so Harriet was as good a person as any. 'I've got a tumour in my eye,' I bellowed over the DJ.

'Tuna?' she replied.

'No! I've got a tumour.' I took a short pause after each syllable to make sure she was getting the full force of my words.

She caught it the second time. She looked up at me and said, 'Oh.'

And that's all I remember. I'm sure she said something more, some nice words of encouragement or support. But I'm also sure she didn't say the *right* thing. I don't know if there is a right thing, or if even adults know what that is. But one thing's for sure: twelve-year-old girls didn't know. That's not because they were horrible or mean, but just because most of us didn't have any understanding of what it meant to be diagnosed with cancer. We didn't have the tools to process the situation, so, much like me, Harriet heard the news and then just got on with things.

From then on, when I told people about the diagnosis I said: 'I have a tumour in my eye.' It felt easier to say 'tumour' than 'cancer'. It was a more manageable situation and sometimes people didn't associate the word with cancer or chemotherapy or hair loss, so I didn't have to endure their sympathy. Sometimes I would add in the word 'only' to play it down further. 'It's only a tumour,' I would say as part of my spiel. It was my way of coping.

Starting treatment

Before I could have my treatment, the doctors needed to perform an operation to put in a Hickman line. I hadn't heard of this, but the doctors explained it was a tube that would go into one of my large blood vessels to give them long-term access to my veins. It would require an operation and a general anaesthetic, something I had never had before.

Once that was over and done with, and I'd had a few days to recover, it was time for me to go back in for chemotherapy. I would need to be in for the full day, but I had no idea what to expect, so I didn't know what to take with me. I settled on packing my iPod.

Sitting on the train up to London, I tried to drown out my feelings with the music pumping through my headphones. A woman tapped me on the shoulder and said: 'You know, your music is really loud!'

I made eye-contact with my mum, then mumbled an apology and turned it down. It just wasn't my day.

At the hospital, I went straight to the oncology ward, where a nurse sat down with me to explain what would happen. As she spoke, a new wave of realisation hit me. I was surrounded by children, many of them babies, all locked in desperate battles against leukaemia and other forms of cancer. It struck me that not everyone would make it, and those who did faced a long and exhausting journey.

The chemo sessions were brutal. I had to head to London every three weeks to spend the day hooked up to the machine, then again a week later for them to monitor my progress and the size of the tumour. I soon became too ill to take the train, so Grandad started driving me there and back.

My body struggled to function under the weight of such potent chemicals, and my system started to pack up. I couldn't eat, and I felt nauseous all the time. When I got home from a session I just had to lie in bed in the dark. I couldn't watch TV because the sight of food made me sick. I felt nauseous just being around any movement. I began to lose weight and my periods stopped.

I had a little bell by my bed that I could use if I needed anything, but mostly I just needed stillness and silence. This lasted for the first week after each treatment, and then for a couple of weeks I was able to function more normally. During this time I tried to see my friends as much as possible and sometimes even went into school.

As time went on, my mental health deteriorated. It's desperately hard to stay positive when you feel so physically unwell. I was offered counselling by the hospital, who referred me to Child and Adolescent Mental Health Services (CAMHS) and made sure I was at the top of the list for treatment. I was grateful for this attention as the waiting lists were long, but I didn't feel I needed it.

I spoke to Laura and Dawn's replacement, Tera, when I was at the hospital, and to me they were like big sisters. I felt I could say anything to them. On one occasion I agreed to speak to a formal counsellor, but as soon as I got into the stale room I clammed up. She asked me how I was doing, and I just said, 'I'm fine.'

Mum interrupted to correct me. 'Liv, you're not fine,' she said in a kind tone, encouraging me to speak.

But I still couldn't muster anything to share. I was low, but I didn't have the words to start to unpack it, especially with a stranger.

My mum has always been my counsellor. During this time we became really close. She stayed by my side every day. I slept in her bed when I got home. I had always loved her, she was my mum, but she also became my confidante and my best friend. I relied on her for everything, and she put her life on pause to be there for me.

The weight of supporting me lay heavily on her, and she also struggled with depression during that time. Mum has always been slim and glamorous, but while I was in chemo she put on weight. It was clear that she put caring for me above looking after herself and maintaining good routines.

My friends were still around, sending messages of support and trying to loop me in on the latest gossip, but I was too ill to spend time with them or even engage with the chat. Before becoming ill I updated my Bebo and Facebook statuses all the time, but I stopped as soon as I was diagnosed. I didn't want to attention-seek or get sympathy. I just wanted to focus on getting well, without the outside distractions. Mum was exactly the same. She didn't offer updates to her Facebook friends or write about how she and I were doing. We closed ranks and kept all our news in the family.

A wing and a prayer

The hospital sent a district nurse to check in on me every day and to keep an eye on my vitals. After I'd had a few rounds of chemo, it became apparent I wasn't doing well. I was vomiting violently and couldn't function at all. The nurse told my mum I was too ill and that I needed to head to East Surrey Hospital in Redhill, where they could monitor me constantly.

I refused to go. I didn't want to be on a ward, which I had grown to hate. All I wanted was the comfort of my mum's bed. But I was deteriorating rapidly. So much so that the nurse told my mum that if she couldn't get me into the ambulance, they would send social workers round who would force me. I didn't have a choice.

At the hospital they decided that I would need a blood transfusion, but I was too poorly to receive one right away. They needed to wait for me to build up my strength, but instead I just got worse. I fell unconscious and the doctors told Mum they thought I wasn't going to make it. I can't imagine what it must feel like to hear those words about your child. It broke her.

They told Mum this would be a good time to say goodbye, so my dad, sisters, gran, grandad, auntie, uncle and cousins all came in to sit by my bedside and speak to me for one last time. They held my hand and told me they loved me while I lay there unaware of anything going on around me.

My whole family was devastated, but Nan responded in the same way she always did when times were tough. She prayed. That night, as she spoke to God about my health, she had the feeling that something wasn't right. It wasn't something she could explain easily with words, but she was deeply unsettled. She felt that God had told her to 'just believe' that I would live. So that's what she did. She kept praying and completely refused to believe that I would die.

Gran got her miracle the following day. I regained consciousness, sat up and started to improve. I fought my way through, and
within a few days was well enough for both a blood and a bone
marrow transfusion, which improved my condition further. I truly
believe that God answered her prayers.

Focusing on the positives

There are so many negatives to contend with when you're having
intensive treatment like chemotherapy. Having to go to hospital all
the time is exhausting, and you start to get sick of the violent strip
lighting, unhealthy food and chemical smell.

Travelling to London was a constant challenge, as I felt so
motion sick. Before Grandad started driving us, other passen-
gers had a go at Mum when I vomited on the train. I understand
that it's not pleasant being around someone who is throwing up,
but I would have expected a little more compassion for a poorly
child.

When Grandad started taking us, he would sit with me and Mum
while I had my chemo, but he would go off halfway through to try
to find me the best lunch ever. I couldn't always stomach it, but I
appreciated the fact that he had walked miles to buy something
special. Then he would drive us home after a long and exhausting
day for all of us. Sometimes the husband of my mum's friend Julie
did the roundtrip to give Grandad a break.

I'm so grateful to them both, but at the time I was angry at the
world, gutted to be missing out on school, and jealous of anyone
who got to feel well and live a normal life. Mum constantly told me
not to worry about school. She wanted me to focus on my recovery.
I could catch up with friends and studies afterwards.

In between treatments, the hospital arranged for a tutor to come
round to the house when I was well enough to have a session or
two, but I dreaded it. I just didn't want to come downstairs. The
tutor ran through the basics of maths and English to keep me up to
date, but no other subjects. I hated it. I didn't want to do sums or
read anything. I just felt so unwell all the time.

That's when my tutor suggested I start writing instead. She encouraged me to write how I was feeling and what I was going through as my English work. Something about the idea of starting a book appealed to me. So I would sit with her and write how I was and what I had done that week, with her correcting my spelling and encouraging me to keep going. I called it *The Story About Me*, and what I wrote became the very first scraps of the book you're holding in your hands right now.

Even a little bit of light makes a huge difference in times of deepest darkness, and there were some positives for me to cling to. Mum stayed by my side every single day. No matter what I was doing or feeling, she was there to lend a supportive hand and talk things through with me. I had to fast for twelve hours before any operation. Mum did the same thing every time in solidarity.

My wider family – cousins, aunts and uncles – just acted normally around me. They didn't give me any special treatment, and they talked about things other than the chemo. That was exactly what I wanted; to be able to enjoy things outside of what I was going through. They clubbed together and bought me a Pandora bracelet with different charms I could add to mark the milestones of my recovery.

Sadly, I was about to face another huge hurdle.

I was about to lose my hair.

7
Bad hair days

People often say the worst thing about chemotherapy is losing your hair. I had been warned on the first day of treatment that this was a common side effect. But the advance notice didn't make it any easier.

It was Laura and Tera who talked me through it. I asked if my hair would fall out all at once, or if it would be gradual. As with many things I was facing, there were no definite answers. They told me it could start coming out after my first session, and that for some people it fell out in dribs and drabs, while for others large clumps fell out at a time. Everybody responds differently.

They even said that some people don't lose their hair, or that it thins but doesn't fall out. This filled me with hope. I told myself I would be one of those people; that my hair was strong and would stay in. I genuinely believed I wouldn't lose it.

However, I started to notice clumps of hair on my pillow when I woke up. That was the most visible place, as it had collected through the night. I would brush it as gently as possible, conscious that any pulling would cause me to lose the precious strands of hair I was desperate to cling on to. I shampooed it as infrequently as I could get away with, knowing that each wash left a significant chunk in the plughole.

One day when I was at the hospital with Nan and Mum, I noticed a bald patch on one side of my head. It was then that Mum said she thought it was time for us to cut my hair. As hair loss stories go, mine is reasonably positive. I had a hairdresser for a mum, so she was on hand to make the best of what I had at all times. Around the same time, singer Rhianna went for a bold, short haircut. She shaved one side of her head and allowed the other side to flop over one eye. I decided to recreate the eye-catching hairstyle.

Watching Mum shave one side of my head was devastating. I was a young girl who, like anyone that age, felt self-conscious and wanted to look my absolute best. She fashioned the style I requested and then we all had to start getting used to it. When I managed to get my strength up between chemo sessions, I would sometimes head out to see my friends.

Shortly after this haircut I went to meet a group in town. Oli was among them, and as I approached, he said, 'What have you done with your hair?'

It was the worst thing I could have heard, and from the worst possible source. He wasn't being cruel; he wasn't like that. It was all said in a playful tone, but he didn't know how vulnerable I was feeling and what a big moment it had been for me to cut off my hair. I laughed it off and told him to shut up. I always did my best not to speak about my illness to my friends, and especially not to the ones I fancied.

My hair continued to drop out, but Mum was ready to help fashion it into different styles each time. I even had a short-back-and-sides at one point before we eventually had to shave it all off. I started wearing a beanie hat all the time to cover up my head, which gave me a sense of comfort.

But it wasn't just the hair on my head that was falling out. Eyebrows, armpit hair, leg hair... it all went. I felt like the woman I had been on the brink of becoming when I started puberty was being ripped away from me. While the other girls were navigating periods, body hair and changes to their shape, I was fighting for my life. I was ready to develop into an adult, but I couldn't – the treatment wouldn't let me.

As well as the various hairstyles, I tried other things to maintain my sense of self. I started drawing on my eyebrows with liner pencils. My make-up skills were undeveloped back then, so they didn't have the delicate look I would have liked. They were dark and heavy, and started far too close to my nose. At one point I even experimented with drawing a slit in them to give me a little extra edge! I took every opportunity I could to express myself through my appearance.

It was Laura and Tera who first spoke to me about getting a wig. If you've never needed to buy one, you don't realise just how expensive they are. At the time, a good-quality, real-hair wig started at £500, and there was no way we could afford that without some help. I was put in touch with the Little Princess Trust, an incredible charity that supports children. The charity provided little surprises and treats that gave me something to look forward to in spite of the horror of it all. They took me to meet JLS and Pixie Lott, and they also organised my first wig.

I was given an appointment at a wig studio in London, and the charity arranged for us to get a train into Victoria and then a cab to the shop. My mum came with me, and we brought my friend Nicole and her mum along, too. The four of us made it into a fun day trip, even though my eye was very swollen, and my hair was thin and falling out in chunks. I didn't look well at all, but I was getting my wig, so I was happy.

As we got off the tube and onto the escalator to go up to the street, a group of girls came down the escalators on the other side. As they spotted me, they started laughing and making jokes. They were shouting that I looked like Sloth from *The Goonies*. Luckily for me, I was excitedly chatting away to Nicole, so I didn't notice. But Mum and Nicole's mum did. Nicole's mum stood next to me with her back to the girls, blocking me from their sight, and Mum talked loudly to drown out their taunts. I'm pleased I didn't hear them, but that moment was very hard for Mum. That was when she realised the nastiness I would have to face. She saw her thirteen-year-old daughter – so excited to be picking up her new wig that she didn't notice she was being shouted at – and it broke her heart. She knew she wouldn't always be there to protect me, and the pain of that was immense for her.

When we arrived at the salon there were lines of seats facing brightly lit mirrors with all the gear you would expect at a normal hairdresser's, but they walked us straight through and into a private room. I was grateful that I would have privacy, as I didn't like taking my beanie off in front of people.

The stylist positioned me in front of the mirror, and we had a brief talk about my hair and the look I was hoping for. I took off my hat and she started fitting different wigs on me. It was like shopping for clothes. I tested out loads of different lengths, shapes and styles. The wigs all started pretty long, as standard, but once I'd selected a light brunette colour that was similar to my natural hair, the stylist cut it for me. I could request a block fringe, side fringe or just for it to be shaped around my face. I settled on a side fringe, but wanted to keep as much of the length as possible. I had always loved long hair, and this was my chance to have it. The ends sat neatly just above my chest, and I loved it. As soon as I put it on, I felt like myself again. I now had beautiful glossy hair, longer than mine had been before my treatment started.

When I think of all the people who helped me during those dark times, I'm amazed by the kindness of strangers. Another charity associated with the hospital bought Mum a new cooker when ours broke, which was amazing. But one of the things that still makes me tear up is the gift Little Princess Trust gave me that day. Not having to shoulder the cost of the expensive wig meant the world to my mum. And getting beautiful long hair back meant the world to me. It was the best gift they could have given me.

I couldn't style the wig in the same way my friends could with their own hair. Slick ponytails were out of the question, and I basically had to stick with the same style every day. Over time, Mum helped me customise the wig so I could continue to creatively express myself through my hair. At one point I dyed it purple, and I also got her to cut in a block fringe. Wigs and hairpieces have come a long way, even in the last ten years. These days it's hard to tell when someone is wearing one, with new glues and systems to keep them in place. But as hard as I tried, no matter how I styled it, mine always looked like a wig.

The wig imposed a few restrictions on the childlike freedom I had previously enjoyed. My friends and I had always gone to the local fun fair when it came to town. Everyone's favourite ride was this cage that spun you around and flipped you over. It was stomach-churning, but we all raced straight there every time.

On one occasion when I was well enough to go to the fair, I had to skip this ride and some others, as my wig was certain to fall off and I couldn't face the humiliation of it. I went home and cried to my mum that I'd had to sit out on so much of the fun, so the next day she attached my wig to my head with her 'tit tape' and took me and my friends back. I rode on everything, including that cage. I was so happy that day. It was one of the best days of my recovery.

I remember laughing once till I thought my stomach would burst when my cousin Lewis put the wig on as a joke for our family, and my sister's friends all loved trying it on when they were round. Sometimes I would leave it on its mannequin in the living room and Mum would get the fright of her life, thinking someone was in the house.

Sadly, it wasn't all positive. Some people were rude to me and called me cruel names. Some made insensitive jokes about my wig flying off. I was able to outwardly laugh off the comments, but inside I was hurt. At times, people wrapped their arms around me when giving me a hug, and would accidentally pull on the back of my wig. Then the fringe would sit higher up on my head, revealing wisps of my own hair underneath. I would have to scramble around to readjust it, quickly tucking any flyaways back under my mane.

On one particularly hot summer's day, I was well enough to go into school but didn't want to wear my wig. It was a period when my hair had started growing back a little, so I had some stubble. This happened from time to time between treatments, then it fell out again after the next session. I knew I would be unbearably hot if I wore my wig over the top. Mum said it would be fine if I just wore my beanie instead. I wore it when I was just going out with family and didn't care about looking nice. So I had to pluck up some courage to put in on for school.

The day was going okay until I went to science class. We had a supply teacher covering, whom I hadn't met before. She had a reputation for being particularly strict with the other students. I sat down, but before starting the lesson she demanded that I take off my hat.

I replied: 'No. I don't want to take it off.'

There was a tense silence in the room. She wasn't deterred. 'You're not allowed to wear hats in school, so can you take it off?'

She was right. The school was strict on uniform and hats weren't allowed, but this was an exception. Surely she understood that, or maybe she didn't know that I was unwell. Maybe no one had told her.

I stood my ground. 'No, I'm not taking it off.'

She just wouldn't drop it and leave me alone; she wanted to know why I wouldn't take it off. I didn't want a scene and I didn't want to announce to the class that I had no hair, but I wasn't about to bare the patchy stubble on my head. The embarrassment of it felt overwhelming. I could have explained properly if she'd taken me to one side privately, but it was the silence of the rest of the class that made me feel I couldn't.

She kept going, insisting that I take the hat off. I took a deep breath and lifted my hand up to my head, but I couldn't do it. In that moment it all felt too much, and I panicked. 'I'm bald,' I said, and burst into tears.

The teacher looked visibly shocked and apologised for being so insistent.

Looking back, I feel for her in this situation. She wasn't mean; she was just doing her job and reinforcing that the uniform needed to be correct, as the teachers at Millais did every day. I can imagine her going home and telling her husband about it that night, and being totally mortified. But why hadn't someone passed on the message so she could have been more prepared and sensitive?

I left the class and called my nan to come and pick me up. During that time, Nan was like my naughty teammate. If I wanted to leave school, I knew she was the one to call. She didn't care what the teachers or anyone else said; she would break me out if I wanted to go home. She was there in less than ten minutes. I left without saying anything to anyone, and an hour later the school phoned her to say that I hadn't shown up to my lesson.

She confidently said, 'Yes, I know. She's with me. She didn't want to be there today.' She hadn't asked me why I'd wanted to leave and didn't bother with any further explanation.

When I got home, I told her and Mum what had happened. Mum was livid and called the school to tell them so. After that, I focused on the home tutoring provided and was reluctant to go back to school.

On another occasion, my family decided to go to Horsham Park for a picnic. It was a sweltering day so, once again, the idea of putting on my wig didn't appeal. Anyone who has worn a wig will tell you that, while it's amazing to have hair again, wearing it for any length of time can get uncomfortable. It was often itchy and irritating on my head, and taking it off at the end of the day felt like removing a particularly tight bra.

I told Mum I didn't want to go, but she dug out one of her silky headscarves and suggested I wear it. I remained reluctant.

'Oh come on,' she said. 'You'll look gorgeous with this on.' Then she proceeded to tie it around my head. It took some getting used to, but I started to come round to the idea that it looked nice.

As we walked to the park, I was convinced people were staring at me. It felt like everyone who passed us by had their gaze fixed on me and what was on my head. Maybe they actually did, or maybe my feelings of insecurity meant that was how I saw it. I've learned over the years to ignore the self-conscious feeling that I'm being watched. Sometimes even when it's true, it's not for a negative reason. If I see someone who looks great, sometimes I'll be staring at them, in my own world, wondering where they got their skirt from. My partner, Max, will poke me and say, 'Liv, stop staring at her!'

Of course, some people did stare at me when I was unwell, trying to work out what was wrong, but it was probably far fewer than I thought. On the whole, people are far more concerned about themselves and what they're doing than the way I look.

Sadly, I didn't have this perspective as a thirteen-year-old going through chemotherapy, so I just felt horrible. I was convinced that I looked awful, but it was fine because it was only my family who would be seeing me.

And then Oli and a bunch of our friends walked by. I was mortified. I tried to keep my head down, hoping they wouldn't see me, but I was hard to miss in my bright headscarf. They beckoned me over and I went to say hi.

As I approached, Oli said, 'What's that on your head?!'

Now, I know this was the second time a poorly placed comment from my crush had sent me home in tears, but in his defence, I came across like I loved the banter. He definitely wouldn't have known how vulnerable I was feeling or how big a deal it was for me to go out that day. All he knew was that we made jokes and took the mick out of each other, so that's what he did.

As usual, I batted his comment back. But as I walked back to the picnic, I could feel my eyes welling up. I asked Mum to take me straight home and, seeing how upset I was, she agreed.

I didn't get much, if any, attention from boys during this time. I had the occasional kiss, but no one expressed an interest in taking me out or being my boyfriend. I don't know why that was. Maybe they just didn't fancy me, or maybe they did but didn't say. In my heart of hearts, I always believed it was because I was bald and wore a wig. I just didn't feel attractive.

Despite all the upsets, challenges and tit tape, I will always be grateful that I got that wig. It made all the difference to me at a time when I felt so ugly and low. When I see businesses that offer this service – some of them for free to those with cancer – it makes my heart feel warm. They are incredible. They gave me back my sense of identity and confidence in myself, and made me feel pretty and girly again. Having the wig made me feel free. I actually looked forward to parties and seeing friends because I knew I would be able to look nice. Wearing the wig made me feel, for a brief time, that I wasn't ill. And that's the best gift I could have asked for.

8

The rollercoaster

After months of chemotherapy and its associated hardships, the doctors gave me the news that no one in this position wants to hear.

'It's not working.'

I felt heartbroken. I'd gone through all that because I believed there was light at the end of the tunnel. I knew that it would be worth it, to save my eye and even my life. But it didn't seem to be making a difference, or at least not a big enough difference.

The doctors told us about a new option they thought might be more effective. It was an intra-arterial treatment. I would be only the eleventh person in the world to try it, which was scary, but I was desperate to try anything that might mean I didn't need more chemo. The procedure involved inserting a treatment tube in through the groin that would work its way up to the eye. Once in place, the tumour would be frozen so it couldn't continue to grow, and I would effectively be cancer-free. It took two sessions to get it in place, and I was under general anaesthetic both times.

Thankfully, the treatment was successful, and a few months later I was declared cancer-free and in remission. This was the news my whole family had been waiting for. The relief was immense, and we finally started to settle back into the routine of life. My hair even began to grow back. Every month after going into remission I took the train to the Royal London Hospital for a scan to make sure the tumour remained frozen. It was usually pretty routine, and I would be in and out within an hour, having been able to take the day off school.

Joy and devastation

On 29 November 2011, eight months after I went into remission, Georgia had a baby. We were all over the moon. It finally felt as if my family was catching a break, as if things were going to be all right. They called him Archie.

Archie needed some treatment when he was first born, so I didn't go straight to the hospital to see him. Mum stayed with Georgia and Archie in the hospital, while Nan kept me and Lauren company, waiting for the call to tell us to head in and meet him.

Mum came home unexpectedly, and she and Nan went into the garden to speak for a while. When they came in, they both looked solemn. Mum looked drained and pale. I immediately wanted to know what had happened. Was there something wrong with the baby? Or with Georgia? It was obvious something had happened.

They sat me down, and Mum told me the Royal London Hospital had called. They said it had become clear at my last appointment that the cancer was growing again, and this time it was aggressive. Before I had had time to process any of that, she said, 'I'm so sorry, Liv. They're going to have to remove your eye.'

That's when the world tumbled down around me like a building that had just undergone a controlled explosion. It felt as if I was sitting among the debris of the life I'd struggled tirelessly to protect. Every exhausting chemo session, every day spent lying still in the dark, every horrific journey home from the hospital, every time I'd vomited, every clump of hair that had fallen out – it had all been done to save my eye. And now they were taking it anyway. The worst-case scenario was about to happen.

I felt so angry. I was furious that they had made me go through all the pain and trauma and it hadn't worked. I could have had my eye removed a year and a half ago, when it all started, and it would have been the same outcome, only without the agony of chemo-therapy. At fourteen, I should have been moaning about school and kissing boys. But rather than making up dance routines to Lady Gaga songs like the rest of my friends, I had just been told that I was going to lose my eye.

I couldn't take my anger out on Mum, as she had completely broken down. The news had hit her just as hard as it had me. For Mum, this rollercoaster of a day had been too much to take. First she'd had the joy of finding out she had a grandson, and then the waiting around to hear if he was okay, and then the pain of this devastating news. I cried with her.

Nan was in tears, too. The three of us sat in the living room sobbing as we tried to come to terms with the news. I had just started to feel I was getting back to normal. I wasn't fatigued, my hair was getting longer, and I was spending quality time with my friends. I had been feeling so positive and healthy that I struggled to believe this news could be real.

I pictured myself with one eye. I imagined walking around with a gaping hole in my face. I thought I would look like a monster with one eye and just a crater where the other should have been. How would I do my make-up? What would be the point? What would people think of me? What would they say?

If I'd thought the staring before was bad, I knew this would be another level. In that moment, I didn't consider the possibility of a prosthetic or that, in many ways, I would still be able to look normal. I didn't know about any of those options. No one at the hospital had talked me through what losing an eye would mean or how I would be supported, because it had always been spoken of as the dreaded worst-case scenario. It was something we had all been united in fighting against. I hadn't needed to prepare myself for it, because it wasn't going to happen – that was the whole point of all the other treatment. Just as I'd started to feel as if my old life was within touching distance, it was snatched away. As far as I was concerned, I would never be normal again.

Sharing my news

Within a week, Mum and I were back on the train to London. It was a journey I knew well and now dreaded. It was the first week of December, and Victoria Station had a huge tree covered in lights and baubles. People were bustling about with Christmas shopping bags. I imagined them going ice-skating or shopping to buy a dress for a Christmas party. It was like my pain meant nothing to them. How could they celebrate? How could anyone be happy when I was about to face something so horrendous?

The doctors were gentle with me, but they reiterated that this had to happen. I would definitely need to lose my eye in order to recover and be cancer-free. They were concerned by the speed at which it was growing, so they told me they would have to act quickly. They agreed to leave it until after Christmas, so I would have one final festive period with both eyes. The surgery was booked in for 30 December 2012.

Happy new year to me.

That night I got into my mum's bed. She put her arms around me as I curled up in a ball and cried for hours. I needed her close, I had to feel her comfort. I was terrified of the surgery and what my life would look like afterwards. I clung to her, holding her as tight as I possibly could.

The first friend I told was Nicole. We were inseparable at the time, and she was constantly at my house. I wasn't the most fun teenage friend to have around – often unwell, frail and sometimes even throwing up out of the blue – but she never seemed fazed or made me feel different. She had come with me to get my wig, and I was about to tell her that I would soon be without an eye.

Nicole was visibly gutted for me, as were Lou (whom I was allowed to see again once I started chemo – our parents agreed to lift the ban as our naughty Year 7 behaviour didn't seem so important after two years of battling cancer) and my cousin Megan when I told them. They were the three people I confided in most. Despite their young age, there was a maturity about the way they took the news. They acknowledged how awful the situation was, but they didn't wallow in the pain of it. They talked me up, encouraged me and pointed out my strengths.

I wasn't able to say much about it, as it still didn't feel real. When they asked how I was, I just said I was fine, but they knew I wasn't. Their support was motivating. Although I had managed to stay positive through most of these trials, I was at my lowest ebb during this period. I had no optimism left, but they managed to find some on my behalf.

Mum was the same. It wasn't easy to see her daughter go through such trauma, especially when it felt unending. But she always managed to muster something that made me feel a little better. I remember her words as I went in for the surgery: 'You will not look bad after this. You're beautiful, and you're going to be fine.' I needed those kind words, and every other kind word from my friends and family.

Celebrating Christmas when I knew my eye was going to be removed a few days later was awful. The day I'd always loved and looked forward to was suddenly covered in a dark shadow. My family did all they could to make it special. Everyone came over and we packed ourselves in around the table, digging out emergency chairs for the occasion. We pulled crackers, swapped presents and ate too much. But I couldn't enjoy it. There was an ominous presence lurking over all of us. It was the eye-shaped elephant in the room.

The surgeon who was set to perform the operation was called Mr Sagoo. Between him and another consultant, Mr Ready, I knew I was in safe hands. We'd had multiple meetings in December to discuss the procedure and aftercare, so I knew what to expect. They walked me through every step of the process. But then again, you can be told all the theory a million times and still not be ready to deal with something so life-altering when it actually happens.

That fateful day

It was my mum, dad, nan and grandad who came with me to the hospital. I took a blanket from my bed at home and my teddy. He was called Teddy Rusty due to his deep-red hue. Ironically, Lauren's dog ripped off his plastic eyes years later during a particularly energetic play session, so Rusty ended up having a lot in common with me.

I was prepped for surgery, which included the nurse drawing a big circle around my right eye with a felt tip, just to make sure they were clear about which was to be removed. I was sitting on the bed in my room when the same nurse popped her head around the door and told me I was next to go down for surgery.

I took a deep breath. It felt like it was someone else getting up to walk to the lift. As we dropped down to the basement floor where the operating theatres were, it still hadn't fully sunk in. It wasn't me doing that walk, monotonously putting one foot in front of the other, because I wasn't really having my eye removed. Something would happen and they would realise it was all a mistake. I would wake up and still have both eyes. I didn't know what was going to change, but I was convinced this wasn't happening to me.

Mum and Dad weren't saying much either – what was there to say? – until Mum looked me in the eye and told me I was going to be okay.

As I sat outside the operating room waiting for the anaesthetist to summon me, Nan prayed. This gave me a sense of peace and calm. It made me feel as if I was loved by something bigger than myself; it was what I desperately needed in that moment. She prayed that I would be kept safe, and that the operation would be successful. She told me God would always be with me and that I would be fine. The waiting room was empty apart from us, so Nan's prayers echoed off the walls and filled the room.

'Olivia, we're ready for you.'

They were calling me in. All the way there, I had felt as if it was happening to someone else, but as I stood up from the plastic chair, it was definitely me. I was going to lose my eye. The first thing people would look at when they met me. A marker of my identity. The signal that I was one of Van Morrison's brown-eyed girls. It was about to be taken away.

In my last moments of having both eyes, I couldn't see straight. Everything was a blur. I walked painfully slowly into the room, like a person condemned to the electric chair. Every inch of my body was feeling the pain and fear. It was soaking into me. I didn't have anything left to fight with. I was defenceless.

The anaesthetist prepared to administer the anaesthetic. These were my last moments of consciousness with both eyes. As with all my previous operations, they asked me to count down from ten. But this time I couldn't. I didn't want to. I was completely deflated. I knew I'd lost the battle, but I refused to join in with the countdown. I wouldn't be complicit in what was happening. The nurse held my hand while Mr Sagoo counted down for me.

10… 9… 8… 7…

And then darkness.

9

Facing my fears

I woke up slowly, sluggishly pulling at my body and tubes, trying to work out what was attached to me. It took me a moment to understand where I was and why I was there. My mind was foggy and there was a searing pain in my head. I looked from left to right and the pain got worse, stabbing into my face. My vision was limited, and I had to turn my head to the right to see anything on that side. I tried to keep my head still and to look directly forwards to minimise the pain. It had happened. It was over. I only had one eye.

My right socket was patched up, and they had put a conformer in where my eyeball had been. This is a clear plastic prosthetic used to keep the socket clean. Mum came in to see me and Dad was there too, but I was in no mood to speak. They stayed by my side, but I couldn't muster any real conversation. I was caught somewhere between the physical pain of the raw optical nerves and my own emotional distress over what I had been left with.

The nurse asked if I wanted to see what my eye looked like now. She said she could lift up the patch and the dressings so I could have a look. I was torn between wanting to know the horror I would be facing and never wanting to look in the mirror again. I agreed that she could bring over a mirror. She slowly peeled back the patch to reveal my exposed skin. I was pleased she did, because what I had pictured was grotesque, but it wasn't that bad. My socket felt far more painful than it looked. Even so, the whole area was swollen and puffy, and as I looked into the void where my eye should have been, I just thought, *I hate myself.*

I stayed in for two nights and Mum stayed with me. This meant spending New Year's Eve in my hospital room. The nurses tried to make it feel a little festive, but I felt I had nothing to celebrate.

I couldn't imagine what the new year would look like without my eye. It wasn't a milestone I wanted to mark.

Mum and I turned off the lights at 10 p.m. and agreed that this was just going to be a crap New Year. I was glad to see the back of 2011, but knew 2012 was set to be even worse. There was no chance I wanted to be awake to welcome it in.

Heading home

Grandad came up to London to collect me on 1 January. I was sent home with strong painkillers, but they didn't do much to mask the agony. It took four weeks for the wound to fully heal, and I didn't look at it at all in that time. I left the dressing on, covering up the socket, to be removed by the nurse during my check-up at the end of January. I was warned not to strain my eye so for the first few days I couldn't even pick up my phone, as the light from the screen was too piercing. I spent a lot of time sleeping or relaxing on the sofa.

Harriet and Megan came to see me and make sure I was okay. Harriet brought round a bunch of flowers and my friend Megan showed up with a Hollister top as a gift. It was the brand we all wanted to wear at that time, so I was touched by the thought – and the cost! Nicole brought me flowers too, and then she just got into bed with me and lay there for a while, keeping me company.

My cousin Megan was a rock to me in those days. She dropped by to check in and tell me all the news about our friends and school. Her sense of humour managed to lighten even the heaviest of moods. At one point I felt so weak that Mum decided to buy me a wheelchair on eBay to help me move around. Megan came with us to pick it up, and then on a snow day she took me to the top of a hill where everyone went sledging and wheeled me all the way down so I could take part.

Navigating the changes

Getting used to the change in my eyesight took time. I was instantly aware of the limit to my field of vision. When people put one hand over their right eye to try to recreate my eyesight, they may see a black section on one side, as if they're watching a telly and the screen's been cut in half and one side is completely dark. But that's not what I see. My brain tells me I have full range in my eyesight, but logically I know that I'm not seeing as much on my right side as someone who has both eyes.

Having only one eye also means my judgement about what is and isn't symmetrical is very skewed. This is most noticeable nowadays when I parallel park. I can pull in and be convinced that I am exactly aligned with the kerb until someone points out that I'm not at all. I've had full-blown arguments with Max when I'm certain my parking is perfect, only to get out and see from a new angle that it's completely wrong. But as I'm only looking out of the left side of my body, things that look straight to me often don't to other people.

After the surgery I was scared that I would never be able to drive, but the doctors reassured me that, when the time came, I would be able to get my licence. I couldn't, however, drive any form of public transport or fly a plane. Thankfully, neither option had made it into my career plan. I would also have to make sure that anyone who got in the car with me knew that I could only see out of one eye, so they had the option to find alternative means of transport if they wanted to.

I've also found that it's far easier for people to creep up on me now that I only have one eye. Obviously, that's not an invitation to try it out! But if someone approaches me from my right side, or if a bird flies by, it takes longer for me to realise they're there. This has led to me being startled by people and objects far more often than I was previously. This usually just results in a good laugh, though.

Another thing I suddenly found I couldn't do was watch 3D movies. Just before my eye was removed, we'd gone to the IMAX cinema in London to watch *Scrooge* on the big screen. It was such a fun day out, so once I had healed from the operation, we decided to go back. This time they were showing *Titanic*. The idea of being immersed in life on the top deck of the famous cruise liner, then being within touching distance of Leo and Kate as it went down, was amazing. As the film started, my sisters were aghast as they fully immersed themselves in the action, reaching hands out to touch things that appeared close by and throwing themselves back as things 'came out of the screen'.

I tapped my mum on the shoulder after half an hour and said, 'Mum, I don't think I can see it.'

She looked confused. 'What do you mean?'

I explained that nothing looked 3D to me. She checked my glasses and they seemed to be working fine, but to me they just made the screen look blurry. Mum and I left, and my sisters finished watching the film. Later, the doctor explained that in order for the experience to work, the glasses needed to change the images going into both eyes to make my brain interpret them as 3D. As I could only send one of those images to the brain, and there was nothing to integrate it with, it wouldn't work for me.

These aren't huge issues in themselves. There are people who have disabilities that cause them far more inconvenience than wonky parking and having to skip 3D movies. But one thing that was hard, especially initially, was that I could so easily compare my new normal to how life had been before. If I'd been born with sight in only one eye, I never would have known the difference, but knowing what my eyesight should have been like made dealing with it all the more difficult.

A huge thing that played on my mind was my one remaining healthy eye. I was terrified that I would damage it, or that my eyesight would dramatically deteriorate. Then I would be completely blind. I'd used up my first life and I only had one left. After that it would all be over. There was no back-up any more, and this terrified me.

I always take extra care of my left eye to minimise any risk. I was advised by doctors not to play tennis or contact sports that could put my eye at risk. I'm not able to wear a contact lens in my healthy eye, as that would increase my risk of infection. But as I began to recognise my fears and work through them one by one, I still didn't realise the worst was yet to come.

Left to right: Auntie Mandy holding Livi just after she was born, with Nan and Mum.

Baby Livi with her dad and sisters Georgia (5) and Lauren (4).

Baby Livi cuddled up with sisters Georgia and Lauren

Livi as a happy toddler (literally) hanging with Uncle Chris.

Livi (3) smiling for the camera.

Posing in a department store photography studio. Left to right: Lauren (7), Livi (3) and Georgia (8).

Livi (9) with her cousin Megan going to a party in a limo.

Livi (10) cuddling up to her mum a year before she received her diagnosis.

Livi wore wear headscarves when she went out with family or friends. Here she is (left) at Toby Carvery with her family and Nicole (right).

Despite the horrible treatment, Livi was offered some amazing experiences. Here, she (left) is abseiling on a trip arranged by the Childhood Eye Cancer Trust (CHECT).

A sailing excursion organised by the hospital. Grandad (bottom left) and Livi (bottom centre) joined the rest of the crew.

Livi at the pub with Nan and Grandad.

Livi having fun on holiday with her friend Lou.

Livi with Great-grandad at a family event.

Posing for a shoot with photographer Zuzu Valla to appear in *Vogue Portugal* in 2021.

At a festival with her friend Lily. Having a photo taken without her prosthetic in while out and about was a big step.

Livi and Max exploring Amsterdam in 2023.

Livi at her baby shower with Lily.

Cousin Claudia just after she had delivered Livi's son, Kaito.

Livi's mum and stepdad cuddled up with newborn baby Kaito.

Livi's dad as the proud grandad.

Max and Livi heading out for an outing with baby Kaito.

Livi posing with Kaito on set.

Beautiful Kaito.

Livi's dad with Kaito (aged 1).

Livi soaking up the sun with her pride and joy.

Livi posing with her mum at a garden party.

Livi all dressed up for the races with Georgia, Lauren and Mum.

Livi posing for a photo with Megan at Megan's baby shower.

10

The eye of the storm

Getting a prosthetic eye takes a long time. Each is made especially for the individual, and it was a month or so before I got mine. Everyone encouraged me, saying the technology was so advanced these days that, more often than not, people wouldn't even realise I was wearing a prosthetic. I was told they used a photo to get an exact colour match and that with the way the new eyes were designed, they even moved around in sync with the healthy eye. I clung on to the hope that this was true. It meant so much to me to look normal again, and I felt that this new eye was the way to get there.

I had no idea what a fake eye would look like or what it would feel like to touch. I took to Google to see what I could learn, which proved to be a big mistake. Sadly, the internet was full of horror stories and pictures of bulbous-looking false eyes. Even the best examples looked odd and fake. Despite my friends' and families' words of comfort and reassurance, I was convinced that my eye would make me look deformed and disfigured.

Anyone who has their eye removed is referred to their local hospital to have their prosthesis made. For me that was East Surrey Hospital. I was nervous to go somewhere smaller and closer to me, where I didn't know any of the staff. Great Ormond Street and the Royal London were so familiar to me. I knew all the staff and they knew me, too.

A couple of weeks after my surgery we got the call asking me to go in and see the technician about my new eye. I was so pleased. We drove over to East Surrey and went to the prosthetics department. I was wearing my conformer to keep my socket clean, and then a patch over the top so people couldn't see that I was missing an eye.

These days I'm confident walking around baring my conformer to anyone, but back then, I couldn't think of anything worse.

We went into the appointment room, where a kind technician beckoned for us to take a seat. She started by explaining a bit about how the eye was made and what it was made of. I didn't take any of it in. I was nodding politely, but in my head I was thinking, *Give me my new eye. Let me see what it looks like!*

She said they would paint it to match my eye colour. I remember asking if they would be doing it that day while we waited at the hospital. To my great disappointment, she explained that she would need to take photos of my healthy eye to get a colour match and a mould of the socket for the shape and size that day, but these would need to be sent off for a specialist to make the eye and paint the iris on over the next few weeks.

The technician then proceeded to take my photo, moving the window blind up and down, testing the lighting until she got the clearest shot. I was disappointed not to be walking away with my new eye, but I was pleased they would be using the photo to paint it. I thought they were sure to create a perfect match.

To take the mould, the technician removed my patch and conformer, and put some sort of plastic balloon in the socket (this is not the medical term!). She filled it with a squeegee kind of paste (again, my words not the NHS's). The paste hardened a bit to a rubbery texture that could be popped out of the socket and used to create my new eye. The prosthetic would then be the ideal fit for my eye and would move in the socket in a way that the previous iteration never had. I felt fortunate to have access to this new, more advanced, version.

It was another month before we got the call to come back for a fitting. The wait was agonising, but I was so excited when the day finally came. They showed me the eye, but it was hard to know if it was right for me before they fitted it. When it went in, I looked in the mirror and was immediately disappointed. My eyes were a light-brown hazel with flecks of chestnut. The iris on this was just a block of brown. It didn't look realistic; there were no veins or variation in colour. It was like a cartoon eye.

Added to that, it didn't feel like it was sitting right. Having never had a prosthetic before, I assumed this was because I needed to get used to it, not because the size was wrong. In time I realised the size was off, which meant that it didn't move around as it was supposed to, and sometimes it became dislodged and ended up 'looking' in a totally different direction from my other eye. I was terrified to touch anywhere near it, for fear of throwing it off centre and looking odd. I forced myself to push through any itch or feeling of discomfort without touching it.

I spent the next two months trying to get used to the new eye, but every time I looked in the mirror, I just hated the way I looked. My self-confidence was completely shattered.

The wake-over

Despite being devastated, I still wanted to get on with my life. I wanted to enjoy the socialising I had missed so much of while I was ill. I always loved that my mum was 'one of the cool ones'. I think she was keen to give me the small pleasures she could whenever I was well enough to enjoy them, so she was always happy for my friends to stay over.

I invited Nicole, Oli and Connor round for a sleepover. Connor had become my best friend and really seemed to understand what I was going through. I still consider him a good friend after all these years. Mum set us all up in the living room with duvets and pillows. We piled them up into a den and then stayed up chatting and playing games.

Eventually, we all dozed off, but I woke up in the night. A couple of others stirred too, and when they looked at me, they immediately realised my eye had been dislodged. These days I would just laugh it off, but at the time I was mortified. I hated that my friends and Oli, my crush, had seen me with a wonky eye.

I held my hand over one side of my face to hide it, and ran upstairs to wake my mum up. By this time we'd made the trip twice before, so we both knew what to do. We jumped in the car and headed to the local hospital, leaving the others to go back to sleep in the lounge. It was 2 a.m., and thankfully A&E wasn't busy.

By 6 a.m. my eye was back in place, and we were on our way home. Mum stopped off at McDonald's to get everyone breakfast. You can see why they thought she was cool, right?

11

Round two

It was three months after the operation that Mum got the call. She was out on the drive when Great Ormond Street Hospital rang, and the news was so shocking that as my grandad came out of the house she collapsed into his arms. We were used to hearing from them, but this time it was different. Grandad held her and cried with her as she prepared herself to break the next bit of disastrous news to me.

Once she was a bit more composed, she and Grandad sat me down. They explained that after my eye had come out, it had gone to a lab to be tested. The medics wanted to make sure that 100% of the cancer was concentrated in the eyeball, and that none was still in my body. The tests concluded that 3% had spread and was still in my body, so I would need to have another round of chemotherapy.

It felt like I couldn't catch a break. Since the beginning of this whole process, nothing had gone my way. At every stage when there had been the potential for bad news, that bad news came. I was starting to feel that nothing would ever come easily to me; that I was destined to have to fight through horrific pain and illness my whole life. I was absolutely broken by the news.

From then on, life was just a countdown to when the devastation of chemo would hit. I spent all my time dreading those four sessions. I had to have another operation so my Hickman line could be put back in. The first session was scheduled for ten days later.

As I was still just fourteen, I went into Great Ormond Street for my treatment. The chemotherapy room was at the end of the ward, with machines and drips lining each wall. They tried to make it an upbeat, happy space with playful colours and pictures on the wall, but I knew what I was walking into this time, so the sunny yellows and bright blues felt oppressive.

Laura and Tera were still on hand to keep me company during the sessions, but this time they got a different Liv. I was beaten and angry. I couldn't believe I was back there. Heartbreakingly, the ward was almost exclusively babies having treatment for leukaemia this time around. So there was no one my age to speak to and bond with. Of course, Mum and often Nan were by my side, but Laura and Tera made all the difference, because they were able to speak to me about normal teenager things. They reassured me that I wasn't missing out and that, in time, I could do all of the things I had dreamed about. They helped combat the feeling of loneliness I was drowning in.

I would eat breakfast on the way in, knowing it would be my only meal of the day. On arrival, the nurses would do my bloods and check my BMI. Then it was time to get hooked up to the dreaded machine.

For the previous round of chemo I had sat there for the seven hours, staring at the bag of chemicals that had to slowly feed into my system. I had watched the monotonous drip falling one tiny dose at a time, willing it to go faster. But this time I was given a different treatment. I had the same bag of chemicals and a second fluid that was bright orange, which had some sort of dye in it. Watching the unnatural-looking liquid seep into my body made me feel like I was going to vomit. It looked like poison. The nurses had to cover it up with a bin liner, just so I could bear to sit there.

Even so, I would start throwing up about two hours into the session. From then, every ten minutes or so I would purge into the hat-shaped cardboard bowl they handed me. Soon I was just dry-retching and bringing up bile. My stomach ached from the muscle contractions. Laura and Tera told me that people were often sick, but it seemed to affect me more than most. They gave me anti-sickness tablets, but they didn't touch the sides.

I constantly had a disgusting metallic taste at the back of my mouth. No matter what I ate or drank, it tainted everything, and I couldn't shift it. I felt so weak during the sessions that I didn't even want to get up to use the toilet. I just sat there needing to go for two or three hours, but refusing to expend my small supply of energy on moving.

I used to say that cancer made me poorly, but it didn't. It was the aggressive chemicals pumped into my body to kill the cancer that made me ill. A necessary evil I had a love–hate relationship with.

The aftermath

On the way back from the chemo sessions, I often felt as if I should eat something. I knew it would be best if I could get some food inside me, even if I just threw it straight back up again. Either Grandad or Julie's husband came to collect us, and we stopped at McDonald's on the way back. It wasn't the most nutritious food in the world, but it was something I could just about swallow. It would all inevitably come back up half an hour later, but I felt that I had made the effort.

When I got home, I would crawl up the stairs and climb into bed. Mum always made the bed and turned it down for me, so it was ready. The big light would be off, and a soft side light would illuminate the room just enough for me to find my way. Then I stayed in there for five days.

After the first session, my hair started to fall out again. I woke up to the familiar sight of matted hair on my pillow. My already short hair became patchy, and once again I had to face shaving it off and wearing a wig.

A district nurse came to the house every day to check my bloods and my chart, and make sure I was doing okay. They were also supposed to change the dressing on my Hickman every four days to keep it clean and fresh. The dressing was so irritating and itchy, I couldn't stand having it there. I wasn't able to bath or swim with it in, so I could only have showers, and I had to position myself carefully so the dressing didn't get too wet.

Every day, I would cheekily ask them to change the dressing, and each day they'd give me a smile and agree. The moment they gently peeled off the tape and my skin could breathe felt like a gift.

At a time when everything felt as if it was clawing at my body, both inside and out, it was a small relief that meant the world to me. They would softly wash it with warm water, dab it dry and redress it. It was the best moment of my day.

Family strife

My relationship with my sisters became strained at this time. They loved me and supported me, but I was naturally difficult to be around. I wouldn't let anyone come into the room unless I'd asked them to. I constantly complained about smells and food and feeling sick. There was a dark shadow hanging over the house, and they could feel it. Of course, they had to carry on with life, going to school every day and getting their work done. But the house wasn't a light place to come back to. I was demanding, and it was a challenge for them, too.

When I called for Mum, I often felt like I needed her right there and then. As I was so sick, I felt the urgency of any request I had. Seeing the toll the whole thing was having on Mum, they felt protective towards her and wondered why I couldn't just wait for things.

There was tension in the whole family. Dad struggled to understand how unwell I was, and often thought I could do things I knew I wasn't able to do. It was like he was in denial, insisting I could walk short distances, even if I knew I couldn't. He would push me to eat food or not to use my wheelchair. He eventually started to realise how little I was capable of and eased up on me, but it took time. Everyone wanted the best for me and for the rest of our family, but it's impossible to understand just how debilitating chemotherapy is unless you've been through it. Not feeling understood became part of the anguish for me. Not being able to relate to others, and seeing that they couldn't relate to me, made me angry.

I knew I had to stick out all four sessions of chemotherapy, to be sure that the cancer was completely gone from my system and there was no risk of it showing up in my left eye. As such a small amount was left in my body, I was told this course would definitely be enough to give me a clean bill of health on the other side. I clung on to that, desperate for it to be true. But by this point I'd been disappointed so many times, I didn't know if I could believe it. I was plunged into darkness, and it felt like there was no light left.

12
The darkest nights

I'd lost a lot of weight from the chemotherapy. I was gaunt and pale. I looked in the mirror, and all I saw was a sick person staring back at me. My bouncy confidence was gone. I'd managed to hold on to much of it through the first round of chemo, but this time was different. I had to lose my hair all over again. I had to feel sick for weeks on end for a second time. And this time I didn't have my eye. There was a hole in my head where my eye should have been, and all I had to fill it was a comically bad static replacement that was liable to slip at any moment.

I was depressed, and I sank into a bleak sense of dejection. I couldn't imagine a life where I would be happy again. Four months into my second round of chemo was the lowest point of my life. The constant hospital trips had taken their toll, and I wasn't coping. My fifteenth birthday was approaching. Added to that, my friends started posting photos on Tumblr of themselves drinking alcohol and planning their outfits for the prom. But not me.

A new low

One evening, I had a blazing row with Georgia. I can't remember what it was about, but I know that we were all feeling the effects of my illness after two years of trying to manage it. I had a breakdown. I felt so hopeless and sorry for myself. I didn't know what I'd done to deserve all of this.

I went into the kitchen, grabbed a knife and started to cut my arm. I don't know why. There was a lot of talk about self-harm at my school, and lots of girls did it. I think I wanted to do something, *anything* that would make me feel. Something that would distract me from all the other painful things in my life, and that was exactly what I wanted.

Georgia saw what I was doing and rushed over to stop me. She snatched the knife from me, furious that I was hurting myself.

When I came out of that manic headspace, I felt ashamed of what I'd done. Mum was frantic. She was worried that because the mark was on my arm, it would be visible. I was at the end of my rope, and so was she. I had gone through so much, and so had she. She wasn't coping either.

No one knew how to deal with me when I had these outbursts. I was just so angry at the world and everyone in it, no one could calm me down. There was nothing they could say to placate me. They couldn't hand me back my eye. They couldn't undo the months of chemo. They couldn't take me to every party I'd missed.

It became harder and harder to lift myself out of these dark holes, and I thought self-harm was a good outlet for my feelings. But these moments of anger added a new layer to the darkness I was feeling, because they made me feel I was to blame. Suddenly I was the bad guy. I was choosing to make the situation more difficult.

Despite all this misery, I still refused to engage with therapy. I didn't want more doctors or more treatment or more experts. I just wanted to be left alone. Nowadays, I know that speaking to someone about how I was feeling would have made a big difference, but I was too young then to know how important it was to push back against that urge to isolate. I see now that there were so many positive ways I could have chosen to process those understandable feelings of pain, but self-harm wasn't one of them. The scars are still visible on my arm to this day, and I feel sad for my younger self every time I look at them.

Unable to pick myself up, I continued to spiral. I felt I had wasted so much time fighting to keep my eye, and I couldn't get over losing it. I had just grown my hair long enough to cut it in a cute, on-trend short style, and then it was gone again.

My lovely wig had been butchered. As my hair had grown out, I'd cut pieces off to attach to hairclips or to create myself a fringe, assuming I would never need the full wig again. The charity kindly funded another wig for me, but I struggled to muster the same excitement about it the second time around.

A couple of months later the aggressive treatment finished, but the feeling of elation I should have experienced never came. I thought I would be happy as soon as it was over, but the depression continued, as rampant as ever. The end of the treatment gave me a chance to reflect on the last few years, and it knocked me back like a tidal wave. I couldn't focus on the future when I was so caught up in everything I'd missed in the past. My mental health declined. Without the motivation of getting through the next chemo session, what did I have? Just an empty life full of decimated dreams. I didn't sit my GCSEs, and as I was behind with my lessons, I wouldn't be able to take them anytime soon.

Everyone else was thinking about college and courses for the future, but I didn't feel like I had one. Everyone was talking about relationships and getting a boyfriend, but no one fancied me. I wasn't pretty enough to get a boy's attention. I was a laughing stock. I was sick of the sympathetic looks and people staring quizzically at my prosthetic eye. I wanted it all to end.

Drastic action

I was lying on my mum's bed one day, where I had slept throughout this time. I decided to take the whole pot of levothyroxine that was sitting on the bedside table. I had been prescribed one a day for my thyroid. I took the bottle and swallowed the pills down, taking swigs of water to help their passage. Then I immediately burst into tears. I cried loud sobs into the pillow. Mum came upstairs to see what was wrong and I told her what I'd done. I didn't want to die. I didn't know what I wanted. I just wanted to stop feeling what I was feeling. I wasn't ready to accept that this was the new me; that this was my life now, and I would have to make the best of it.

Mum was in a frenzy. She grabbed her phone and called for an ambulance. I didn't lose consciousness, but just lay there crying while we waited for the paramedics to arrive. They were in the bedroom within ten minutes. It was two women who came to treat me, and they were incredibly kind and friendly. They explained that I shouldn't have taken the pills. I felt a wave of embarrassment that they had come out just to speak to me because of what I'd done. It hit me that there were other people out there who were also at breaking point, but I was taking up their time with something I had inflicted on myself. It was all my fault.

They performed an assessment on me. I felt funny having taken all the tablets, but not in pain or unwell. The women explained to Mum that these pills wouldn't have had a huge impact, unlike some others. They still took me to hospital, where I was monitored for any adverse effects as they waited for the pills to pass through my system.

After that, I was put back in touch with the therapy team, where I was encouraged to talk about how I was feeling. But, as before, I clammed up. I found it too hard to talk about, so I only attended a handful of sessions. Once again, this is something I deeply regret not investing in more.

Mum was terrified and furious in equal measure. She couldn't believe I had deliberately overdosed after all we'd come through, after we'd sat through all those miserable chemotherapy sessions and the various operations. As far as she was concerned, the worst was behind us, and we could finally start to rebuild our lives. From where I was standing, I couldn't imagine ever feeling happy again.

Mum was so desperate for me to look ahead and see what my future might hold. Thankfully, she was right.

13

A fresh pair of eyes

After my final chemotherapy session, I was given the all-clear. They had told me I would be cancer-free after these treatments, but I hadn't allowed myself to believe it. I didn't dare to get excited before it was all official, but then it was. Even when I was told, I struggled to celebrate. I still felt so ill that I didn't have the energy to mark the occasion. Still, it was a relief. I was so grateful that I would never have to go through the pain and nausea of chemotherapy again.

Once I had recovered from the final session and was back on my feet, Nicole, Megan, Lou and I threw a party. I invited my sisters and my whole group of friends to the house, and we had drinks and food and danced around all night. I put on my wig, applied some make-up and covered my Hickman line with a big patch. I still missed my real hair and hated my prosthetic eye, but for once I felt pretty. I was paranoid about dislodging my eye, so instead of looking left or right, I tried to just move my head instead. It wasn't ideal, but just for that night I didn't care, because I was finally cancer-free!

One of my neighbours came over and complained that we were being too loud. Nicole's mum took her to one side to explain what the party was for, and the neighbour eased up and said the music was fine.

After that, I went into hospital to have my Hickman line removed again. It was such a relief to be rid of it and the irritating dressing. I could finally go swimming and have a bath. When I got home, I filled the tub with hot, soapy water and soaked in it, fully immersed for an hour, just because I could. I hadn't realised how much I would miss something so simple until it was taken away.

A new prosthesis

The final annoyance was my awful prosthetic eye. I tried to have it updated so it was more consistent with the other eye, but it still didn't feel right. East Surrey Hospital sent it off to have some veins and a better depth of colour added to the iris, but it was still wrong. Aside from the colours, the shape was uncomfortable. I tried for months, but I just couldn't get used to seeing it as part of my face.

During a session with Dr Kingston, I told her how bothered I was by the prosthetic eye. She'd asked me how I was doing, and I just blurted it out. 'I'm so unhappy with my eye,' I said. 'It doesn't look like me. Is this what I'm always going to look like? Will I always feel unhappy?' I told her it made me feel more self-conscious, and I was doing all I could to hide it away and cover it with a fringe. She saw how deflated I felt and how much the eye was getting me down.

That's when she referred me to Moorfields Eye Hospital in London, the leading eye specialists in the country. She told me that if I was willing to travel up there, they would fit me with a whole new eye there and then, on the same day. She said if it didn't fit, they would change the shape, and if the colour wasn't right, they would repaint it. She told me I wouldn't have to leave until I was happy with the eye. I couldn't believe that I would get that opportunity. I suddenly felt a glimmer of hope.

Fresh hope

Two weeks later I was back in London, but this time I was pleased to be there. I had an appointment with the prosthesis specialist at Moorfields and I couldn't wait. This was the first time I had enjoyed a hospital experience. The eye they made me was spectacular. It looked just like the one I'd lost. I couldn't believe how beautifully they matched it to my eye colour. As soon as I put it in, I felt like me again. I felt like I finally had my big brown eyes back.

Getting my life back

As the weeks ticked by, and I got my appetite and some of my colour back, I started to feel a new lease of life. Having an eye that made my face look more like mine made a huge difference. Along with my face, I felt I had got my personality back. I could smile again, and I made jokes with my friends and sisters. My confidence slowly started to build, and I stopped feeling the need to cover myself up.

Once my hair had grown a few inches, I ditched my wig once again and Mum cut in some short styles. We dyed it silly colours, shaved the sides and had fun with it all over again. Not only was I starting to look and feel like my old self, but I was regaining my strength, both physically and mentally. I knew that life would never be the same as it was before, but I felt positive about what I could make of my new normal. My resilience grew, and the silly teasing from Oli and my friends was far easier to shrug off and laugh along with. It was important for me to build my resilience, as not everyone would treat me and my differences kindly.

On one occasion I was round at Lou's house. She and her boyfriend got into a blazing row about something, things got heated and they started to square up to each other. I jumped in the middle, trying to defuse the situation and encouraging them to take a breath. He backed away and said: 'Shut up, you one-eyed prick.'

It was the first time someone had so blatantly insulted me because of my eye. I'm sure people had made remarks behind my back – I was probably the talk of my year at school. I didn't like that idea, but often those kinds of comments come from a place of curiosity, not viciousness. But this was different, and to me it felt cruel.

I took myself out of the situation and went home. I felt gutted. I was so sad that someone would speak to me like that, as if my pain was a joke or a tool they could use against me. Hearing those nasty words caused me to take a few steps back, and once again I had to focus on rebuilding my confidence. I didn't get involved in their arguments again, and I stopped sticking up for her for fear of what he might say to me.

That incident aside, Lou and I got on really well. I built a new relationship with her parents, too, and loved being at their house. They became my second family. It was the only place other than my own home where I could walk around without my wig on. Her dad was so supportive and always made me feel as if I looked great. He treated me normally and made silly dad jokes. I made a whole new group of friends where Lou lived, in the little village of Southwater, and we would all hang out and have fun together. It felt like a fresh start for me in my new world, and I began to enjoy life again.

A little while later I was heading to the cinema with Mum when I got a call from Lou's boyfriend. I didn't usually speak to him directly, so I was surprised. I picked up and he sounded out of breath and panicky. Lou's dad had died in a car crash, and she wanted me to come straight away. I got that sick feeling in my stomach that only comes when something horrendous happens.

We ditched the cinema tickets, and Mum drove me straight over to Lou's house. As we pulled up, Lou opened the front door and stepped out onto the street. She looked empty. Tears were falling from her face, but she couldn't speak through the agony of her grief. She fell to the ground. I knew what it was to feel pain, but I didn't know what to do. I hadn't been around anyone in such acute mourning before. I felt helpless. I just hugged her and cried with her.

Just as I was putting the pieces of my life back together, hers was falling apart. Her family couldn't cope with the tragedy, and Lou's relationship with her mum deteriorated to the point where, at fifteen, she came to live with us. My mum couldn't stand seeing her so upset. She wanted Lou to have a safe place to process what had happened, so she took her in. Lou shared my room, and I was pleased to have her close. We both had things to process, and we were able to lean on each other in unique ways.

After a year or so she moved into the YMCA, which meant she qualified to go on the council list for a flat. She was given one not long afterwards. I felt sad seeing her stay in that hostel when other people had ended up there as a result of abuse, crime or addiction. She was just a young girl who had lost her dad and whose relationship with her mum had broken down. These days she's well rounded, fun and an incredible mum. I'm so happy to see how happy she is, especially after everything she supported me through and then went through herself.

14

My new normal

Finally happy with my new prosthetic, and having been given the all-clear, I was able to start getting used to living my new normal. As a person's eyes stop growing at five years old, I'll be able to keep my new prosthetic for the rest of my life. For babies who have ret-inoblastoma, they need to have their prosthetic updated regularly, but that won't be a problem for me.

This means that looking after my false eye is a priority. I still have awful daydreams that I'm cleaning the bathroom and it drops down the plughole, never to be seen again. Every eighteen months I take it back to Moorfields Eye Hospital, where they polish it up and make sure it's still in perfect condition. They do this while I wait, and I only have to hand it over for half an hour before it's back with me, good as new. At the same time, the doctors will check my left eye to make sure I'm still cancer-free and there's nothing to be con-cerned about. In most instances this stops after ten years or so, but as mine was such an unusual case, they've asked me to keep coming in every eighteen months for the rest of my life, just to be sure.

The way a prosthetic eye is maintained varies from person to person. At night, I pop it out of its socket and soak it in a saline solution. Sometimes I sleep with it in, in which case I just slip it out to clean it, and the socket, in the morning. But I've spoken to some people who don't take theirs out at all. A man I spoke to left his in and cleaned the whole area with a damp cotton pad. I usually prefer to sleep without mine, as it feels more comfortable, but as time goes by I have been keeping it in more often.

Sometimes when I'm not feeling well, or if something's got into the socket, the socket becomes puffy and bloodshot. If that happens, I pop out my eye for a few days to allow the swelling to go down. When I used to go out with friends for a messy night, I often woke up with lots of gunky sleep around my prosthetic. I realised that drinking alcohol made my eyes a little drier, so I needed to give my eye an extra clean the next day. Hangover days usually involve leaving my eye in the saline solution now.

Getting back out there

The regular removing and cleaning of my eye became a self-care ritual I enjoyed. It was nice to feel that my routines were healthy and helped me to thrive rather than just survive. As I grew in my confidence and started to feel more like myself, I started to venture out more with friends. This meant I got to enjoy more of the normal teenage experience you would expect for a fifteen-year-old… but it came with new challenges.

The first date I went on after going back to school and trying to get back to normal life was with a boy from Forest School. Halfway through the date, he stopped, gazed at me and said, 'Your eyes are so beautiful.'

I was taken aback by the compliment. I didn't know what to say. I was still getting used to my eyes, and I wasn't prepared to have someone comment on them. I thought he was taking the mick out of me – that maybe he knew about my eyes, and someone had made a bet with him that he couldn't compliment me on them. I couldn't work out if he was being kind or mean, so I left. On reflection, I doubt he was trying to be rude or wind me up. It's possible that he knew and was trying to reassure me, or didn't know at all and was trying to be romantic, but at the time I felt too embarrassed to stay.

I was once at a house party when I had a falling out with a friend. We were both throwing around insults, and I said things I'm certainly not proud of now. When I moved away from her to talk to somebody else, she attacked me and smacked my face onto the floor. I left and called my nan to pick me up, but while I was waiting outside, she punched me in my eye socket and pulled my hair.

A fair number of people have similar stories from their teenage years. Of course it's not okay for people to shout at and insult each other, but the level of violence that night was horrific. The pressure from the punch to my socket dislodged and disfigured my prosthetic, which meant a trip to the hospital to have it checked out. There was a haemorrhage in the socket, and it took weeks for it to look normal again. And it was heartbreaking when a chunk of the hair I'd been so excited to see growing back was pulled out of my head. Incidents like this would rock any teenager, but I was more vulnerable than people realised. It took a lot for me to pick myself back up after that fight.

On another occasion, a group of us went down to the skatepark. It was a popular place for our friends to hang out during our collective emo phase. I showed up with Lou, and there was a lad there who was known for being hard work. He was often angry and didn't mind upsetting people. In fairness to him, he went through a lot as a child, but it didn't make spending time with him any easier.

My hair was growing back, but it was very short. He came over and said, 'You look like a boy.'

It was such a simple, silly statement but it felt like a crushing blow. I kept my composure and just replied, 'Well, I'm a girl.'

He didn't seem to accept my response. 'What the hell's wrong with your hair, then? You literally look like a boy.'

For some reason he needed his opinion that I resembled a boy to be heard by everyone around us. He wouldn't stop, he just kept repeating it over and over. Seeing that he wasn't planning on leaving us alone any time soon, Lou stepped in. She was one of those fiercely protective friends. The kind who shouts at people for you, in the way that you would only do yourself when you play it back in your head later. She wasn't having it. She told him to go away – but in stronger terms.

A while later I went to another house party. It was Lou's boyfriend's group of friends, and one of his mates was throwing the party. From what I could see, his friends were very similar to him, so I found them immature and difficult to get on with. Because I didn't hide my disapproval of some of their behaviour, they weren't keen on me either. I went to the party anyway, as everyone else was going.

I showed up with my friend Mia. Everyone was drinking and chatting and listening to music when, later in the night, I got into a bit of a debate with one of the boys in that group. I stopped enjoying the party, so Mia and I decided to leave.

As we walked out of the front door, this boy followed with some of his friends. There were already thirty or so people standing out in front of the house, chatting and smoking. I continued to walk away, and he shouted, 'Oi, you one-eyed idiot. You look like a cyclops.'

Everyone turned around, and some people did an overdramatic 'Ooooo', as if they were watching the prefight trash talk between two wrestlers.

Teenagers all have silly arguments and fallouts; it's part of growing up and learning to get on with one another. But when people brought my eye into it as a way of insulting me, that's when I was reminded that I was different. That was when I realised that, to them, I would always be the girl with one eye. I would never be normal.

I went home and cried to my mum about what had happened. She was upset for me and angry at him. But it was my sisters who got the most fired up. They couldn't believe someone had spoken to me like that, especially in a situation that was so unequal. He had come out with a crew of mates just to insult me. I was with just one friend, trying to leave. It wasn't a fair fight.

In 2022, I was having lunch with my family at a pub when one of the girls who had been part of that group came over to apologise to me. She said she was sorry for how she, and everyone, had behaved towards me. It felt good to hear that, but I didn't really need it by then. I'd moved on. We ended up having a drink together and catching up for an hour. We all do stupid things when we're kids. I'm grateful when other people give me the benefit of the doubt, so I like to do the same.

I've often thought back to those incidents when people were rude to me. I was driving my nephews around a few months ago, and we went past the skatepark lad who had said I looked like a boy. He's not a lad now; he's a man driving a white van. It's funny how there are loads of people from around that time that I would never remember, especially people I had so little contact with. But I remember him. I remember his full name and what he was wearing that day. It's seared into my brain.

I told my nephews the story and explained that they should never be people whose names stick in someone's head for the wrong reasons. Maybe I'm just the annoying auntie trying to teach teenagers about the importance of being nice. But it is important, and I do want them to be nice. To everyone.

Taking positive steps

The one positive that came out of the bullying I experienced was that, when I got older and felt more secure in myself, it was comments like those that motivated me to speak out. I didn't want other young people to suffer the way I had because people were ignorant. I wanted them to see that I was proud of my prosthetic, no matter what nasty comments other people had thrown at me.

There were also many fun times. Once, my friends and I were all messing around at breaktime, and for some reason we were sitting in the toilets. We were laughing and joking, and I popped my eye out. Everyone started screaming and running around, and soon we were rolling about on the floor laughing. It became a joke when a new person started hanging around with us that I would offer to let them hold my eye. People were fascinated by it and had loads of questions. But I felt safe answering them with my good friends, because I knew they were asking from a place of love. Being able to speak openly about it with those closest to me formed a big part of my learning to accept myself and how I looked. Having spent so long trying to avoid the subject during chemo and hoping people didn't know what was going on, it was freeing to finally open up to my closest friends.

After a while, I wanted people to know that my eye was a prosthetic, as I preferred that to having them wonder if I had a lazy eye. I started to feel empowered by my story, and it became important for me that people knew my eye was a symbol of overcoming, not of weakness. Sharing became something that helped me to cope.

My mental and physical health continued to improve, so I decided to take part in a sailing event to raise money for people with cancer. Mum, Nan and Grandad all came down to the Isle of Wight with me and we made a day of it. I sailed with some other kids who had been diagnosed with cancer, and we all shared our stories. It was moving to hear how far everyone had come, and sad to see that others still had much further to go. It was humbling.

The actual sailing was great fun. Mum and Grandad came with me, but Nan waited on the shore. Grandad had a thing for fresh air and the open water. He loved it, so the outing was right up his street.

They invited us up to steer the boat one by one. Not knowing how to captain a sailing boat, I turned the wheel full throttle to the right – or the starboard side if we're using the official lingo. The whole thing tilted to one side, and Grandad went flying towards the water. He was pressed up against the rope railings, the only thing between him and the water. Four of the crew members rushed over to pull him back to the middle of the boat, while another grabbed hold of the wheel to steady us.

Grandad, bless him, is a little stocky, so it took them a few moments to get him back to safety. Meanwhile, he had his hands in the air shouting, 'Just let me go!' because he would have preferred to be one with the water!

When the whole ridiculous scene settled, and I had apologised for the mistake, Grandad reiterated that he would have been very happy in the water, but apparently with all the propellers and other boats, it wouldn't have been safe. So that was the day I almost killed my grandad. Thankfully, he forgave me!

The hospital arranged for me to be taken out sailing a few times over the years, and I absolutely loved it. They taught me how to manoeuvre the boat, tie the ropes and hoist the main sail. I was always strapped in with a harness, so I never had any near-death experiences like Grandad, but I always think fondly of those outings.

Make-A-Wish offered to pay for any wish I had when I was first diagnosed with cancer. I asked to go shopping in the big Topshop on Oxford Street, and I got so many new clothes. They sent a limo to take us there and back, and even paid for dinner after the shopping spree. When I received my second cancer diagnosis, they asked me what I wished for again. I had enjoyed the first trip so much I asked for the same again – and I wasn't disappointed!

My story got some press coverage in the local papers. By this time I was sixteen and well on my way to recovery. The *West Sussex County Times* and *All About Horsham* magazine did interviews with me and wrote about what I'd been through, but I was most excited when we got a call from Channel 4.

They sent a full crew round with cameras, giant mics and a presenter to record an interview with me. It took a whole day, but the piece was cut down to a few minutes on the actual show. I was just amazed that people wanted to hear about me!

15
Looking for love

When I got the cancer diagnosis, I became the girl who was unwell. I didn't date, and people didn't show much of an interest in me. I would often opt for being funny over being fancied, and was quickly 'friend-zoned'. Maybe that was for the best – it's not like I would have been a very fun teenage girlfriend at the time – but I couldn't help but feel jealous of my friends who kissed guys and changed boyfriends every week.

Dating Ben

Despite my crush on Oli, he never became my boyfriend. We just stayed friends, and he was part of the tight-knit group who were very supportive on my good and bad days. After the chemo, I struggled to see myself as very likable, but my confidence began to grow, and suddenly Ben came along.

It was the first week of college and I was seventeen years old. My hair had grown back, and I was getting used to life with prosthetic eye 2.0. I was finally feeling better in myself.

I was leaving the lunch hall one day when I saw Ben walking over to what we all called smokers' alley. He was wearing a beanie, baggy jeans and a denim jacket. I immediately thought he was fit. I asked one of my male friends if he could introduce us, and Ben and I ended up swapping numbers.

He was the first person I properly dated. We went to house parties together and enjoyed sneaky kisses in the corner. Being with him was exciting. He walked me home from college every day, so I invited him inside to meet my family, and I met his.

I was so excited to be seeing someone, and to be accepted for who I was, that I was keen to move things on to the next stage and officially become boyfriend and girlfriend, but Ben never wanted to put a label on our relationship. This was why things eventually turned sour. He wanted to hang out with his mates, and I wanted a proper boyfriend, so things just fizzled out. But I stayed good friends with him and his whole group.

My first boyfriend

I got into my first relationship when I was eighteen years old. I was on a night out with my friend Megan in Horsham, walking towards a bar we all used to go to called Mungo's, when we bumped into a girl we knew. She was with a guy I'd never met before. He was a bit older and had an air of confidence about him. He introduced himself as Nathan, and asked where we were going. The four of us ended up having drinks together, then I went off to a club with some female friends.

I didn't think much more of the encounter, as he lived a little way away in Reigate. I assumed I would never see him again, but then I woke up with a hangover and a text from him the following day.

After that we were messaging non-stop. He was twenty-one and I loved that he was a bit older than me. He worked as a graphic designer and dressed like someone who had an eye for style. I was besotted. We had so much in common, and started going out soon afterwards.

By the time I turned nineteen I had my first official boyfriend, and he and all his friends and my friends came to celebrate my birthday in my garden. I finally felt I was worthy of being in a relationship. It felt amazing to be picked by someone after watching all my friends couple up over the years while I was ill.

He would go into London for big club nights that his friends organised, so suddenly I was thrust into a new and exciting social scene. For me, it was special because I had always hated getting the train to London. I associated it with feeling nauseous and getting bad news. But now I was reclaiming the city. It wasn't just where I had spent my darkest days; now it was where I spent fun nights out with my boyfriend.

I hadn't enjoyed college, so after switching things around and trying a few different courses, I decided to drop out entirely and get a job. I started working as a carer, which was hard work and long hours, but I had a pay cheque and my own money to spend. I loved being able to treat myself to outfits and go to the London clubs at the weekend.

An unhappy ending

Sadly, the honeymoon period with Nathan was short-lived, and we started to argue more and more. Over the three years we were together, we broke up several times. While we were on a break, I saw pictures of him on Snapchat cosying up to other women, and he wouldn't reply to my messages for days on end. We didn't just break up for good because we were both young. I didn't know what a good relationship looked like, and I cared about him so much. I forgave a lot because I really wanted to be with him.

One time he went on a lads' trip to Tokyo, and I had a feeling something went on while he was away. He eventually confessed to having slept with a girl while he was out there. I was so upset; I couldn't believe he had cheated on me. We had a blazing row and I broke up with him, certain that would be the end of our relationship. Only it wasn't. He was persuasive, and it wasn't long before I had picked what I thought was love over self-respect. I guess this is the kind of mistake we all make when we're young.

Things came to a head when I accidentally fell pregnant. I was twenty-one at the time and had no plans to have a baby with Nathan. I told my mum and she said she would be supportive of any choice I made. Georgia had her first child at the age of nineteen, so I knew it was achievable with a supportive and loving family.

Nathan wasn't so gentle about it. He was clear that there was no way he wanted a baby. When I said I wasn't comfortable having an abortion, and I would have the baby without him, he told me I was being selfish and should take his preferences into account. Even his mother got involved, sending me messages telling me I was making the wrong choice. In the end, neither of them needed to worry, as I miscarried the baby.

I was only nine weeks pregnant when I started bleeding one afternoon. I rushed to the hospital and Nathan came with me. They gave me a scan and the midwife told me there was a big blood clot next to the sack, and things weren't looking good. I had to have a procedure to help me pass the foetus, which was difficult and painful, but Nathan stayed by my side.

Our relationship wasn't the same after that, and we ended up going our separate ways at the start of 2018, when I was twenty-two. Despite all the arguments and infidelities that so often come with young love, I'll always be grateful to Nathan. When he first found out about my eye, he asked a lot of questions. He was forward about it and didn't shy away from the topic. He was kind and never treated me any differently because of what I'd been through.

Nathan was the first person to suggest that I talk about my experiences on social media, and that my story might help other people. He taught me a lot of the skills I needed in order to build a social media platform, which has connected me with many amazing people and opened up incredible opportunities in my life. He was the first person to take my photo without my prosthetic eye in. He didn't push me to post it, but suggested that I might want to in time. He made me feel accepted and beautiful despite my differences, and even though he wasn't the perfect partner, I will always feel grateful to him for that. My best friend Lily also encouraged me to speak out openly about my prosthetic and to go public with photos, as she thought it would help me mentally and physically to do so. I wasn't up to it at this point, but I felt it might be something I could be open to in the future.

Romance at a wedding

I waited a while before I started dating again. I needed some time to regroup and heal after all that had gone on. Sometime later, I was at my cousin Sian's wedding when I met Alex. My cousin Megan – Sian's younger sister – introduced us, and we kept catching each other's eye throughout the night. He was super good-looking, and took centre stage when we all hit the dancefloor. I was drawn to how carefree and happy he was. At first I was a little put off, as he was three years younger than me, but Megan insisted I shouldn't worry because he was mature. He worked for his dad's construction company and already had his own car. We started following each other on Instagram and then on Snapchat, and in no time we were constantly messaging. He was fun and flirty, and the conversations were exciting.

We set up a double date with Megan and her boyfriend, and I remember feeling nervous on my way there. I knew Alex was easy to get on with, but I felt I had to tell him about my eye straightaway. If it was going to be a problem, I wanted to know sooner rather than later. He told me no one would ever know I had a prosthetic eye if I didn't tell people, and was always comfortable with me taking it out and walking around without it.

Turning up with Megan gave me the boost I needed. We went to Top Golf, and Alex drove to my house to pick the two of us up. He pulled into the driveway next to my little Ford Fiesta. He was in a brand-new BMW. I'd only seen cars like that as prizes on game shows! His position in his dad's company meant he was well off, but he was also funny and easy to talk to. He had a beautiful singing voice, which really attracted me to him. We laughed a lot.

At the end of the date he dropped Megan and her boyfriend home before driving me back to mine. Once he'd parked, he leaned over and kissed me.

Afterwards, I rushed straight into the lounge and told Mum and Lauren that we had kissed. They wanted to know everything, so I sat with them and told them every detail from start to finish.

Alex and I carried on chatting, and soon we were dating. He brought me roses every time we met up, and within two weeks of our first date had asked me to be his girlfriend. He was part of a warm and welcoming family that completely embraced me from the first day we met.

Alex lived in an annexe next to his family home, so it wasn't long before I moved in and we shared the little house together. We were young, but living together made me feel like we were adults. It was like playing house, but instead of plastic cups and plates, everything was real.

Everything was going really well… apart from one snag.

On our first date, he'd told me he had booked to go travelling for six months. It had always been his plan and the flights were already paid for. The timing was awful, and even though we'd known the plan, we had still allowed ourselves to get serious quickly. He offered to help me pay for the trip so I could join him, but it wasn't what I wanted. He even considered reducing the length of his trip because he didn't want to be away from me for too long. He was due to fly out in March.

We celebrated New Year's Eve together at a party hosted by a friend of my mum's. At about 10 p.m. my phone pinged with a message from a number I didn't recognise. It said: 'Happy New Year. I'm thinking of you. I miss you.'

I had no idea who it was from. When I asked my mystery messager, I got a one-word response: 'Nathan.'

It set my head spinning. From then on, Nathan continued to message, and I felt so confused. I loved Alex, but he was leaving – and I had always felt so drawn to Nathan. I couldn't handle the uncertainty of it all, so I broke things off with Alex not long before he flew out on his trip. He was heartbroken.

At first, he refused to accept it. He said it was abrupt, and it was. I deeply regretted hurting him. He had treated me so well, and I allowed myself to call things off because I was in a tailspin.

I tried speaking to Nathan for a while, but it never felt right for me. By the time I realised I'd made a big mistake with Alex, he'd started dating other girls. I apologised for what I'd done, and we did agree to give things another go. But then he left for his big adventure, and dating him while he was travelling put a strain on our relationship. Given what had happened when Nathan was abroad, I struggled to trust him.

His messages became fewer and further between, and eventually he told me he didn't think it was right that we carry on. He was discovering himself, and there wasn't a place for me in his life.

It was hard to hear. I bitterly regretted messing him around, but I had to accept that he didn't want this any more. Things were frosty between us when he first got back, but we do still bump into each other from time to time, and he seems happy in a new relationship.

A bad influencer

After that I went on dates with a few people, but nothing really stuck. I met an influencer at a fancy London club night and we hit it off. We started messaging back and forth on Instagram and decided to meet up for a date. He lived in London, so I agreed to jump on a train to see him, but then he said he'd booked us a hotel room. I was apprehensive about this addition to the evening, but decided that, as he was reasonably well known and we'd been chatting for a while, it should be fine.

The day before the date, I did a complete 180 and decided I definitely didn't feel comfortable staying in a hotel room with him. I dropped him a message to say that I had changed my mind and would have to cancel. He'd sent me the booking confirmation for the room, and it clearly said he could cancel within twenty-four hours without paying a fee. I made sure he had plenty of time and even offered to pay if there were any charges.

He hit the roof. He wasn't understanding at all, and was offended that I didn't want to spend the night with him. He sent me several abusive messages telling me to f*** off and ended with him calling me a 'pirate c***'. I couldn't believe what I was reading. His social media platforms were all about lifting others up and being kind. But underneath it all he was rotten. He thought it was acceptable to insult someone who'd had childhood cancer just because they didn't want to have sex with him. I was disgusted, but also pleased at my lucky escape. I told him how ashamed he should be of his response and blocked him before he could send over another barrage of childish, hateful messages.

16

Becoming an influencer

It was just after Christmas 2020 that I posted my first picture without my prosthetic eye on social media. It was the one Nathan had taken of me. I was really tanned and had ashy-blonde hair cut into a bob. I wrote a long caption, mentioning those who might not be enjoying the festive period, and reflecting on my experience all those years previously when I was in hospital preparing to have my eye removed after a long battle with cancer. I added:

> Try not to get caught up with materialistic things because I can assure you they will never come close to health and happiness. I thank God for another year spent at home with family. I wasn't always so lucky as I am now. Things change and things do get better in life. Keep your head up and try to stay positive even in the darkest of times.

I was proud of the message. It felt like a positive contribution to all the Christmas content that was out there. At the time I only had around 800 followers, so I wasn't expecting a big response. Even so, posting it was nerve-racking, and I was apprehensive about the reception. I took a deep breath and then made it live.

I couldn't resist checking the reaction regularly, and within a day it had 700 likes – more than I'd ever had before. The comments section was flooded with positive messages. There wasn't a single troll.

I had assumed I would get some mean comments, like the ones from when I was younger, but I was met with love and support. Seeing the impact my message and picture had, I started to feel empowered to continue speaking about my experiences. It is so rare for someone to be diagnosed with retinoblastoma at the age of twelve. I was only the second person in the UK to have received the diagnosis past the age of five. The other was a man who had been seven at the time.

This means that very few people have any memory of the cancer or the treatment. I was in a unique position to be able to shed some light on the trials and challenges on behalf of children who wouldn't have been able to express themselves and what they needed fully. It was a gift, and something I could pass on.

Positive feedback

What blew me away most was that I started receiving messages from other people who'd had an eye removed or the loved ones of children having treatment for retinoblastoma. A lot of people who contacted me had lost an eye for a completely different reason. Many thanked me for the honest post, and suddenly I started to connect with others who had been affected by the same cancer.

The stories of resilience people share with me have blown me away and inspired me in equal measure. And when someone isn't doing so well, I'm pleased that I can reassure them that, in my experience, it will get better. I didn't always feel positive about my future, but I can see now that there's so much ahead, and I want to help others see the same thing.

I continued posting, and over the years my following grew. Sharing how I was feeling and connecting with others online became like therapy for me. Social media helped me to rediscover myself and my voice. Even Mum says that I've come out of my shell since the day I posted that first picture. I no longer hide my eye, try to cover it with my fringe or look at the floor when I interact with new people. I slowly stopped dreaming of having two eyes again and started enjoying my life with the one good eye and the incredible prosthesis I had been blessed with. My eye is no longer an insecurity, and that's something I never thought I would be able to say.

I've had comments from people saying things like, 'My young daughter has a prosthetic eye, and when she grows up I'm going to show her all your videos.' It warms my heart. The feeling is so humbling and I'm proud that I can do that for another person, because I didn't see anyone in the media with one eye when I was younger.

Wider reach

Soon my posts were gaining attention and people were starting to notice what I was putting online. My old friend Harriet, the one I first told I had cancer at that under-18s disco all those years ago, dropped me a message to say that she was working on a mini documentary as part of her university course, and she wondered if I wanted to share my story.

I agreed to take part, and a whole crew came over to my house to record the short film. Speaking about the most painful parts of my life made me feel vulnerable, but it was also the right time and the right person for me to do it with. Harriet knew me, and knew where the boundaries lay when it came to what I wanted to discuss. I trusted her, and she put me at ease, which has helped me so much in front of the camera over the years. She was confident, but also gentle in the way she posed the questions. However, despite her caring approach, running through the story from start to finish was an emotional rollercoaster. It was like I was stripping myself down in order to do it. I spoke about the diagnosis, the chemo, the operation and my recovery. I also shared some of the nasty things people had said to me about my prosthetic eye.

I was proud of the documentary when it came out, and was excited to share it on Instagram. It quickly gained attention, and I was blown away when I saw that 6,000 people had liked it.

Not long after that I got a direct message from Katie Piper. I couldn't believe it when I saw her name pop up in my inbox and assumed it must be a scam. I checked the account and forensically examined the message. It actually appeared to be from her. I'd been a fan of Katie's for years. I remember the moving documentary she made about her own life-changing event. I remember thinking I would like to share so honestly myself one day. I loved how she embraced her differences. To me, she was a role model. I had always wanted to help people in the way that she did.

Katie's message said that she had seen my story on Instagram and that I was an inspiration. She initially thought I had lost my eye due to a burn, but then she'd watched the mini documentary. She said she thought I was amazing and strong, and that she'd followed me partly because of my story and partly because of my style!

It was a 'pinch me' moment. I couldn't believe that *my* inspiration was saying that *I* was an inspiration. I was so awestruck, I didn't know what to say, so I asked Mum how I should respond. In reality, I didn't need to get in my head about it, as Katie was so kind and warm. We messaged back and forth for a bit.

A while later I was doing some cleaning work for a lady called Fiona who lived in the area. We were chatting about it, and she said she was close friends with someone on Katie Piper's team. Fiona reached out to her friend, and before I knew it, Katie got back in touch again to invite me to join her on her *Extraordinary People* podcast. I couldn't believe it.

This was my first big interview. I had really enjoyed recording the documentary, but it was emotionally heavy, and I'd had to dig deep to share some of the more upsetting parts of my story. By contrast, speaking to Katie felt light. We talked about the trials and challenges, but she focused on the positives.

A helping hand

I couldn't help but feel blessed to have so many supportive friends and family members, both while I was unwell and while I was adjusting to my new normal afterwards. They were by my side through the chemotherapy, the hair loss and the sickness. But there would always be a disconnect between our experiences. As much as they tried to put themselves in my shoes, they could never know what it was really like to lose an eye.

That's where the support of the Childhood Eye Cancer Trust (CHECT) was invaluable. A member of their team, Lesley, was in touch with our family, and when it became clear that I would lose my eye, she introduced me to Megan. Megan was a twenty-one-year-old woman with beautiful long brown hair and only one eye. She had lost her eye as a baby, and wore a prosthetic. But rather than letting it inhibit her, Megan was happy. She made the most of every moment and lived life to the full. It was the first time I realised I could potentially do the same.

My phone calls with Megan had a huge positive impact on my mental health and the sense of hope I felt for the future. So when CHECT asked me more recently if I would become an ambassador for the charity and support other people in the same way, I immediately said yes.

I started going into hospitals to meet children who were having their eyes removed and to speak with their parents. It's emotional and difficult, but I draw so much strength from it. When it feels like my world is crashing down, I'm able to stay grounded through these meetings. They remind me how far I've come.

It's a privilege to be able to offer comfort and practical advice to people who aren't sure how to navigate such a difficult situation. I can't tell people not to feel down – that's a natural reaction – and I needed to feel my own emotions in order to move through them. What I can offer is a reminder of the inner strength that each of those children and parents has, and an encouragement to keep going.

I also speak to support groups and adults who are living with prosthetic eyes. When I first started, I was surprised by how many people were ashamed about having only one eye. Plenty of people I met would never have taken a photo without their prosthetic. And plenty more had never taken it out in front of another person. I met a woman who had been married for thirty years and never removed her prosthetic in front of her husband. I felt sad that she had hidden it away. I don't see living with a prosthetic eye as a secret that others should be shielded from; I'm proud of my differences. I encouraged that woman to try to show her husband this side of her. I knew that if she could just show herself in all her vulnerability, it would only deepen his love for her.

Saying goodbye

In winter 2021, around the time that I was visiting hospitals and my modelling work was kicking off, my great-grandad passed away. Most people don't get to have a relationship with people three generations above them in the family, so I knew I was blessed to have known him. He had lived many years without my great-grandma, and had always been a big part of our family life.

Great-grandad was ninety-five and very independent when he died. He had gone out on his mobility scooter to buy a newspaper and hit a pothole. It sent him flying and he hit his head on the pavement as he landed. He was concussed after the fall and had no memory of it. After that, his health rapidly deteriorated. Nurses started going into his house daily to check in on him, but quickly decided he needed to go into hospital for treatment. He was desperate to go home so he could be at peace in familiar surroundings.

As this happened during the COVID pandemic, there were restrictions on when we could visit him, but I managed to get to the hospital to sit by his bed. His eyes were flickering, and he wasn't able to speak to me. I played his favourite song on my phone, and he gently opened his eyes. I held his hand, and he gripped mine back. The following day, I got the call to tell me he had passed away.

Hosting an awareness day

Between the documentary and the podcast with Katie, I started attracting even more followers and connecting with many others who had been through similar trials. It was as a result of those conversations that I decided to host an awareness day.

Having had so many inspirational conversations with people who had survived retinoblastoma, I had the idea to bring them all together for one event. I wanted to host an awareness day at a lovely venue, where they could all meet each other and we could build a network, but also so we could record their stories and use the footage to show in schools to raise awareness.

In 2021, I gathered ten people from across the country for the day. They all agreed to join me at a venue in Essex that was kindly donated by my employers at the time. Young children came with their parents, alongside teenagers and adults, to take part in the day. Nine had prosthetic eyes, while one still had his eye, but also had a condition that meant he might need a prosthetic in the future. Not everyone had lost their eye due to retinoblastoma, but everyone had similar stories of adjusting and overcoming with one eye.

The day was phenomenal. Seeing so many inspirational people in one room was more warming than my heart could cope with. Katie Piper even recorded a special message for all the guests. We mixed and mingled, but some people were shy – particularly the younger ones – and took a while to warm up and share their stories.

I hired a friend of a friend to take footage and asked him to conduct interviews with each person, which could be edited into a documentary that I could package and show in schools. Sadly, I made a mistake with my choice of videographer. He took months to send over the footage, and when he did, the interviews were barely audible, as he had relied on the built-in camera mic rather than bringing his own. I was gutted when it became apparent that the documentary we had tried to make wasn't going to work. Especially after all the time, effort and money that had gone into getting everyone there.

I emailed the others to explain what had happened with the footage, and I really felt I was letting them down. But each person was so kind, saying that they had taken a lot away from the day even without the video, that I felt encouraged. My dream is to reshoot that video one day, and to create something that will educate and inspire others.

17

A new career path

It wasn't long after I featured on Katie's podcast that modelling agency Zebedee got in touch. Its founders, Zoe and Laura, slid into my DMs to introduce themselves and, if I'm honest, I once again thought it was a scam. I'd had 'agencies' message me before, but in reality all they wanted was for me to shell out for a pricey portfolio. I was all geared up to delete the message when I read on and saw that Katie Piper was one of Zebedee's ambassadors, and they had found me through the podcast.

I agreed to do some test shots and, on seeing the results, they confirmed that they wanted to sign me. It was surreal seeing my pictures on their website along with other big-name models – including Ellie Goldstein, the first model with Down syndrome to pose for high-end fashion brand Gucci.

Once I was signed up, things started to move quickly. Within ten days they called to say I had my first job. It was the co-founder Zoe who called me to let me know. 'Do you want to know who it's with?' she asked.

I imagined myself modelling clothes for a catalogue or maybe a small shop on the high street.

'It's *Vogue* Portugal!' she said.

I couldn't believe it. I dropped to the ground and burst into tears. After all the miserable years of feeling left behind and unattractive, I was going to be featured in the most famous fashion magazine on earth.

Two weeks later, Mum and I jumped in the car to make the familiar trip up to London, but this time I couldn't wait to get there. We headed to a studio on the outskirts of the city where I met my photographer, Zuzu Valla. She is internationally recognised, and fights hard to get more visibility for disabled models. We hit it off straightaway, and I instantly felt at ease.

They had a make-up artist and stylist on set. The stylist pulled out the outfit I would be wearing – a Dior dress. It was a blue, floor-length number with sequins. I'd never seen such an expensive item of clothing. My whole wardrobe was from River Island and H&M. The fabric felt thick and luxurious. When I put it on, I felt like a queen. I was in a dream world. Mum sat on one side of the room watching. She looked as if she was going to cry at any second, she was so proud.

I got a few more modelling jobs after that, including one for Premier Inn. My photo was featured on their booking confirmation emails for a while, which was a fun addition for any friends or family who stayed in one of their rooms.

In between jobs, there were plenty of exciting calls or emails from Zebedee telling me I was in the running for a project that didn't come to anything. It's always disappointing when the casting team decides I'm not right for something, but I do my best not to get my hopes up.

It was in January 2022 that I got another opportunity. Zoe emailed me to let me know that I was in the running for a Primark campaign. She explained a bit about the job, which was modelling Primark's new lingerie line, but what caught my eye most was the fee. I couldn't believe how much they were offering to pay their models; it was more than I normally earned in six months as a cleaner. It was hard not to get my hopes up when I knew how much of a difference the pay cheque would make.

I called Mum to tell her: 'Mum! They're considering me for Primark! I *need* to get it!'

She replied, 'No, you're *going* to get it!'

I loved how much confidence she had in me. Talking to her always gave me a little boost.

Off to Manchester

The following week I got another message saying that I was down to the final six for the job and I had to go to Manchester for a fitting. Primark would do a test shoot with all the potential models, then pick three for the campaign.

Travelling alone, I got a train to London, then changed onto a fast train to Manchester. Primark had arranged for a taxi to pick me up from the station, so I found my cab and jumped in. As I had been booked to model without my prosthetic eye, I quickly popped it out and stowed it away in its case during the journey. I often did that on the way to a job. I wonder if the cab drivers notice that I get in with two eyes and get out with one!

I hadn't done a casting before, and felt anxious at the idea of it. I pictured a group of women who all starved themselves and were bitchy to one another. In reality, there wasn't a celery stick or a side-eye in sight. They were all so friendly and welcoming, I felt right at home. The models and the team from Primark were chatting away, and I enjoyed getting to know everyone.

The stylist fitted me in some of the bras from the latest collection, and when it was my turn I posed for a few photos. Putting on the underwear was exciting and nerve-racking. I had my insecurities like anyone else, but on the whole, I liked my body. But liking your body in the mirror at home is very different from liking it in a photography studio under the bright lights. I modelled Primark's smooth cup, skin-coloured range and a white lacy bralette with matching knickers. Everyone on set was so kind and made sure I and the other models felt comfortable. I left the shoot feeling empowered and hopeful that my openness and confidence would inspire others.

Once they had seen all six of us in front of the camera, the casting team took half an hour or so to chat, and to call through to the Primark head office, to confirm the choices. Finally, they told us which three girls they had picked... and I was one of them! I couldn't believe it! I was screaming inside, but reacted calmly as we were told in front of the three models who sadly hadn't been picked.

I stuck around for the night, and they put me up in a lovely apartment. It was twelve floors up with amazing views of the city. I had my own kitchen and living room, and a bedroom with a massive king-sized bed and ensuite. I FaceTimed Mum to give her a tour of the flat. I felt like I was living in another world.

The shoot

On the day, the three of us put on all the different lingerie sets and spent the day posing for pictures. The crew also captured some video content for their social media platforms, so we had a real laugh messing around in front of the camera. The photographers complimented me on my ability to fake laugh on command, and the shoot went really well.

It took a few months for the photos to start popping up in the Primark stores. My pictures were visible in twelve countries, and friends started sending me photos of myself on posters in various stores. A few months before I finished writing this book, I saw some of my photos in an Amsterdam Primark during a trip there.

After that, I was keen to make modelling my full-time job, but it didn't work like that. The opportunities came in waves, and as it's so competitive, there were plenty I didn't get. So now my attitude is that it's a privilege if I'm given a job. I never went out of my way to become a model, so anything I'm offered is an amazing bonus.

My dad is my biggest fan. Every single shoot I do goes straight up on Facebook, proudly declaring that I'm his daughter. I love that he and my mum are so encouraging.

I'm also really grateful to Zebedee for the way they champion people with differences. We're slowly seeing real change in the modelling industry, with increasing numbers of disabled models landing big contracts. A lot of that is down to Zebedee and the way they raise awareness. I'm so proud to be a part of their agency, and for my own little contribution to this important effort.

18

Living life to the max

Once I had healed after my operation, I did my best to cram in as much socialising as possible. I wanted to make up for every conversation I'd missed and meet every new person I came across. I had some catching up to do. My friendship group grew quite quickly, and one of the people who joined it was Max. He was part of a group of lads who lived in Crawley. They would come over for house parties and we would hang out together at weekends.

Like most teenagers, the midweek communication between us happened over Facebook or Instagram. This was back in the day when people were still writing on each other's walls and confidently exchanging messages even if they didn't know each other very well in real life.

Max and I were just friends. He was the kindest of his group of mates. He wasn't a big flirt or attention-seeking at all. He just liked having fun. He was carefree in a way that lots of other boys weren't. He didn't seem to need to prove himself. No one disliked him, and he was known for having a sweet soul.

I thought he was great, but when we first met I was desperately trying to let my hair down, and was heading into a bit of a hectic period with parties and dating, so I never considered that I would end up going out with Max. He seemed too gentle for me.

The years went by, and we continued to hang out. When I was about sixteen, Mum went out with her then-boyfriend one night. I assumed she would stay at his that evening, so cheekily took the opportunity to have some friends round. Everyone was drinking, chatting and smoking just as Mum walked back through the door. She was shocked when she saw that I had thrown a party behind her back and immediately kicked everyone out.

That was the first time Mum met Max. He had hidden in her bedroom when she unexpectedly came home, then decided to make a dash for it, bolting towards the back door and then having to vault the garden fence to escape. As he ran past Mum, she shouted, 'Who are you?!' but he didn't stop to introduce himself. Thankfully, our friendship survived the forbidden party. Our group of mates continued to spend time together, but the hangouts became fewer and further between as we all moved into adulthood. I eventually lost touch with a number of people in the group.

It was in the year after my break-up from Alex that things changed between me and Max. I gave myself plenty of time to heal, as it had been such an intense relationship, and I was sad it had come to an end. Around ten months after Alex first went travelling I decided it was time for me to get myself back out there.

I was scrolling through Instagram when I saw a familiar face in my 'suggested profiles' section. Instagram was suggesting that I follow Max. I clicked on his page but could only see his profile picture, as he had his privacy settings turned on. I was pleased when I saw that he was already following me, so I followed him straight back. Once he had accepted my request, I could see his photos. I ran through them and couldn't help noticing how good-looking he was. In a modern move to get his attention, I liked a few of his pictures and hoped he'd get the message that I was interested in chatting. He liked some of my pictures back, so I thought we were on, but after a few days he still hadn't started up a conversation. I realised that if I wanted to speak to him, I would have to kick things off. He just wasn't the forward type.

I went with a flirty, slightly sarcastic comment: 'I thought I would say hi. Otherwise we're gonna be liking each other's pictures and never actually talk.'

It went down well, and he replied, asking how I was. These days he maintains that he was just about to message me that evening to get things going, but I got in there first. Convenient, huh?

Not long after that we went for a drink, and the conversation flowed so naturally. We never struggled for things to say. I felt really comfortable with him. I liked that I didn't have to tell him about the cancer or my eye, because he already knew and he clearly didn't have any issues with it. He made me feel secure and attractive.

After a couple of cocktails we decided to go somewhere a little livelier. We went to a club where a few of our mutual friends were out for the night. We did shots and carried on chatting. By about 11 p.m. we were on the dancefloor, getting increasingly close as the music and drinks muddled together, helping us to drop our inhibitions. And then he leaned in and kissed me.

From then on, we were inseparable. We couldn't stay away from each other. There was no doubt that we both felt strongly about each other, no game playing. We just enjoyed being together. I was Max's first girlfriend and he treated me like a queen. It was really refreshing to be with someone so genuine and caring. He made me feel so happy.

Max is half Japanese, half British. His mum moved over to the UK from Tokyo years ago and met his dad here. I was introduced to his family and instantly got on with them. Max was an only child, so his mum hadn't had a girl around to balance out the male energy. It was fun to chat with her about fashion and clothes, and all the things Max didn't take much interest in.

I quickly felt settled with Max. All of the pain of previous relationships fell by the wayside, and I stopped thinking about anyone else. We sometimes bicker, but on the whole we communicate in a kind and healthy way. A year after meeting we moved in together, and not long after that, the two of us became three.

19

Mum life

Max has never been a great lover of kids. There are some people who insist that they want a whole football team of children, but he isn't one of them. As an only child, he doesn't have any nieces or nephews, so he isn't close to any children. He's a fantastic partner, and I always knew he'd be an amazing dad, but it certainly wasn't his priority, or even in his plans at all.

I stopped getting my periods when I was on chemotherapy, but they started up again when I went into remission. I always struggled with heavy painful periods and needed various treatments over the years. When I started using oral contraceptives, my body didn't respond well to the hormones. I had mood swings and bled constantly. After a few years of trying different types, I came off them altogether.

When I started seeing Max, I didn't restart the pill, but we made sure we took other precautions. After a year and a half together, we moved into a lovely little cottage, just the two of us. We were committed to each other, and we both knew we weren't looking for anyone else. It was so exciting to have our own space, we became a little more carefree.

We had been out on the town one night for my dad's birthday. It ended up being a late one, and we stumbled back home after a few too many drinks. Things got steamy and we woke up tangled up under the bedcovers and severely hungover. There were a few life stresses about our relationship hanging over us at that time, so when I started to feel nauseous a few weeks later, I assumed I was just rundown. When the feeling didn't subside, I decided to take a pregnancy test.

When the second line developed on the little screen, I couldn't believe it. I was pregnant. Max and I were having a baby! He was at work, so I called him to break the news. He was lost for words. All he said back was, 'Wow.'

He came home from work, and we sat and talked about what having a baby would mean for us. I was twenty-five at the time, so we were young, but not *that* young. We were strong, and we knew that we had a loving home to bring a baby into. It didn't feel like the perfect time to have one, but I'm not sure there is ever a perfect time.

I told Mum next, as I tell her absolutely everything. She congratulated me and was so excited that she would be a grandma again. Max went to tell his parents in person. When I saw them a few days later, his mum came over and gave me a massive hug. His whole family was so supportive of us.

We gave up the tenancy on our little cottage so we could find a baby-friendly place. While we looked, I moved back in with my mum, and Max moved back with his parents. That meant we could save a little before the baby came. When I was seven months pregnant, I moved into his family home so I could be with him in the final weeks.

My pregnancy symptoms were reasonably mild. I went off meat and couldn't stand the smell of cigarette smoke, but otherwise things were pretty straightforward. Even so, I wasn't one of those women who love every second of their pregnancy. Towards the end I started to feel exhausted. It was tiring carrying around the extra weight.

At eight months I stopped working and stayed home to prepare for the arrival of our baby boy. When Max came home from work, I was usually still sitting in bed. He'd ask if I'd been there all day, and I confirmed that I had, aside from my shower and a few loo breaks. He always picked up a meal deal for me on the way home, so I would be sitting in bed watching *Selling Sunset* on Netflix, excited for him to come back so I could tuck into my BLT and prawn cocktail crisps.

My due date was originally set for Christmas Day 2023, but when the baby was measuring small, they pushed it back to 13 January. In the end I went into labour on 6 January. I was lying in bed with Max when I started having contractions. They were mild at first and far apart, but they soon began to increase in both pain level and frequency. I couldn't sleep between them, and by 6 a.m. I was having a contraction every four minutes.

I woke Max up and told him to call my mum. She was my birthing partner, and along with Max would be by my side in the delivery room. She drove round to collect me, and we all bundled into the car with my birthing bag, which was waiting by the door.

After that my contractions started to become less predictable. They came thick and fast for a while, then slowed down to ten-minute intervals. When we got to the hospital, they died down a bit. A midwife took me into triage to examine me and said that I was only one centimetre dilated. I was desperate for her to be winding me up, but sadly it was true. I was nowhere near ready to give birth. She told me it was likely to be the following day, so I should go home and try to rest.

We went back to Mum's house. I dosed up on painkillers and tried to ride out the contractions. By 4.30 p.m. I was really struggling to keep going. Mum, in all her wisdom, decided it would be lovely for Nan, Grandad and my sisters to come by and see me at this special time. So it was like the worst Sunday lunch ever, with everyone checking in on me while I screamed my way through the agonising contractions. Nan prayed with me and stroked my hair. She didn't like seeing me in pain – no one did.

Mum ran a bath in an attempt to relax and soothe me. I got in and she started washing my hair, but I couldn't stand it. I knew I needed to get out immediately. I felt claustrophobic sitting in the warm water. I got out before Mum had a chance to fully wash the shampoo out of my hair. The water had also smudged my make-up, so I looked a bit like a ruffled Nessa from *Gavin and Stacey*.

I knew I needed to go to hospital, so I told Mum to take me in straightaway. She phoned the hospital, who told her they had checked me and I was only one centimetre dilated, so I should stay put. But I knew something was wrong; I knew something was happening. The contractions were every two minutes, and I couldn't take it. They agreed that I could come in for a pethidine injection

– a strong painkiller that would hopefully help me through the worst of the pain.

I lay down in the back of the car while Mum drove and Max was in the passenger seat. I was doing my best to pant through the contractions. Max, obviously nervous and unsure of the protocol, started asking Mum about her plans for the weekend, and if she was going to see either of my sisters. I lay there, amazed that he could be engaging in small talk while I was in so much pain that I felt I might pass out.

It was as we pulled up to the hospital that my waters broke. I felt the warm fluid soak through my clothes. Max jumped out of the car and came running back with a wheelchair. I sat in it, and he pushed me in the direction of the maternity ward while Mum went to park the car.

I clung on to my pregnancy pillow as he manoeuvred me through the corridors. We found the lift, but I couldn't wait any more. I couldn't sit on the chair. I got up, placed my pregnancy pillow on the floor, and lay down on it in the middle of the corridor. Max looked startled. In an urgent but hushed voice, he said, 'Liv! What are you doing? Get up!'

I screamed back, with none of the same discretion, 'I can't! There's no way I can move!'

I told him to go and get me a bed. He didn't know where to go to get hold of a bed and pleaded with me to get back in the chair so we could go two floors up to be seen by the midwives. I just couldn't move. There was no way I could sit on the chair. Mum rushed around the corner to catch up with us, just in time to see the stand-off in action. Everyone wanted me to move, but I stood my ground and insisted that it just wasn't going to happen.

Eventually, because I was causing a blockage in the hallway, someone went away and brought back a bed for me to go up to the ward in. By the time we got to the labour ward, the team was moving with some urgency. They took me into a private room and the nurse asked me to move onto the other bed so she could examine me. I told her I physically could not move. There was no way.

I think she thought I was being dramatic, but even so she decided to humour me. She came over and began the examination while I was still on the mobile bed. Within seconds she pulled back and shouted for someone to take me straight into the delivery room, as she could see the baby's head.

Mum grabbed her phone and messaged my cousin Claudia, who was a midwife at the hospital and was on call at the time. She drove down and came straight into the delivery room with me to help me have the baby. By the time I got in there I was told it was too late for me to have any kind of pain relief. I was given the consolation prize of gas and air, which did absolutely nothing.

I had asked Max to set up his phone to film the business end of the proceedings so we would always have a record of when our baby took his first breath. When I watch it back, I'm always caught off guard by just how scarecrow-like I looked with my half-shampooed hair and panda eyes. It was all just part of the magic of childbirth.

The actual birth took just twenty-five minutes, and my cousin told me I was the loudest of any woman she's helped during labour. With a final push and a shrill newborn cry, we had our little boy. Max isn't a weeper by nature, but even he teared up when he held him for the first time. We called our baby Kaito.

Having always felt horrible in hospitals, this experience felt redemptive. Don't get me wrong, I didn't enjoy the process – but the outcome was well worth it. It was nice to reclaim my memories of hospitals and actually enjoy being in there after the birth.

Unlike Max, I had been around babies most of my life, as my sisters and cousins all had children. I knew I would be good at the practical things, like changing nappies, but I also knew I would be a good emotional support for my little one. Initially, though, it wasn't easy to bond. I hadn't felt particularly connected to the baby while he was in my womb. I wasn't one of those mums who speak to their bump or anything like that. When he was born, I knew I loved him immensely, but even so it took a little while for us to bond. I've often wondered if I had mild postnatal depression, as those first weeks after he was born were very difficult. But then I was also dealing with extreme tiredness and a whole new routine, so there were plenty of things rocking the boat.

Since having Kaito, he's become an unending source of joy, but also my motivation. Knowing that I want the best for him pushes me to be a better person and a better mum. It also inspires me to work hard, so I'll be able to give him great opportunities in life and so he'll be proud of what his mum achieves.

A major worry during my pregnancy was that he would have the same retinoblastoma that I had, and would need to have treatment and potentially his eye removed. It can be transmitted genetically, so although it was unlikely, I knew I wanted to have him checked as soon as he was born.

I was actually offered a check while he was still in my womb, but I turned it down. I didn't want to go through the pregnancy knowing my baby had cancer. I just wanted to have the tests when he was born and deal with whatever came then. I put off informing the hospital of the pregnancy, even though they had told me to keep them in the loop from the start if it happened. I didn't want to face the idea that my little baby might have to experience what I had. I told my medical team when I was eight months pregnant, and we agreed that I would take him to the Royal London Hospital for tests when he was three weeks old.

Max had to work that day, but Mum was keen to come with me. It was Mr Sagoo who ran the tests, the same surgeon who had removed my eye all those years ago. I felt certain my baby was in safe hands with him.

While he was checking Kaito, he introduced me to a trainee doctor who was working with him. This man already knew all about me, as my situation was so rare. Mr Sagoo told me he often uses it as a case study in his teaching. He said he had come across the documentary about me online and was so proud of all I had achieved. It felt overwhelming to hear that from one of the people who had saved my life.

We waited for the results, and the doctor confirmed that Kaito was clear. He was at no heightened risk of having retinoblastoma. It was such a weight off my mind to know that he didn't have any traces of the cancer and there would be no need for regular check-ups.

As things stand, there are no additional challenges for me as a mother with a prosthetic eye. But I'm conscious that, down the line, Kaito will have a lot of questions and school can be a difficult time for any child even vaguely associated with someone who is different. But Max and I will teach Kaito to be kind and not to put people with disabilities down. We're going to focus on teaching him to see each person for the unique individual they are.

Being a mother has given me a whole new appreciation of the pain my mum went through when I got my diagnosis and had chemotherapy. To see your child suffer through something so difficult, knowing there is no way to take the pain away, is more than I would be able to bear. But she stayed strong for me and my sisters, and for the rest of our family. I am in awe of her.

20

On the positive side...

At the time of writing, I've been in remission for twelve years! There was a day when I couldn't imagine being able to say that. I'm so grateful for the life I have now, and I celebrate every single milestone. Each year on the anniversary of receiving the all-clear, my family gathers together to mark the occasion. The family WhatsApp group is buzzing that week.

The pain of it all has allowed me to appreciate the simple pleasures that are so important in life. It's been a long journey for me to feel comfortable in my skin and love my differences. I spent so long hating my looks and feeling jealous of everyone around me. I would look at girls with long hair or sparkly eyes and think that their beauty dampened mine. But these days I know that's not true. I love my differences. My scars and prosthetic eye are a symbol of all I've overcome. I look at them now and feel happy.

I also draw strength from my faith. Every time I pray with my nan, I feel a wave of peace coming over me. Even though I wasn't religious as a child, faith has become increasingly important to me. I believe that God has been watching over me. When my family was called into the hospital to say goodbye to me, the doctors really thought it was my last day. There was no medical reason for me to have improved so much that by the next day I would be able to have a blood transfusion. To me, that was a miracle answer to my nan's prayer as she stood at my bedside. She just had this assurance that I was going to live and not die. That's what kept me going, and ultimately helped me to heal from the trauma of having cancer. These days I start and end my day with a prayer, just to say thank you for all I've been given and to stay connected to God.

When I look at the paths life has taken me down, it's clear that there have been no coincidences. Every inch of my experience has been used to build up my resilience and wisdom, and I've been able to pass that on to others who are struggling in the same way I did. Seeing how other people are impacted when they witness the hope I have for the future moves me more deeply than anything I've been through. I was surrounded by loving friends and family throughout my treatment, but I still felt alone. It's an isolating thing to go through. So to be able to reach out a hand in the middle of that, and say, 'I understand. I've been there too,' is invaluable. I'm grateful to every person who supported me, and I'm proud to be able to do the same for others.

These days, I feel positive a lot of the time, and I try to focus on positivity on my social media platforms. But that doesn't mean I don't have down days. There are occasional days when I would rather just stay in bed or on the sofa. We all feel like that from time to time, and it doesn't mean we're not strong. It's strong to recognise our limitations and to be gentle with ourselves, but we can't let ourselves wallow in them. That's what I've learned. I give myself time to feel the pain, and then I keep going.

I think everyone has the opportunity to be a role model. There's always someone a little younger or a couple of steps behind in their journey who is looking for examples of how to cope. For me, it's been other people with prosthetic eyes like Megan, women like Katie Piper who empower other women, and all my friends who never stopped showing up for me. But my biggest role model is my mum. I will never forget the way she sacrificed everything for me. She never left my bedside.

Challenges will come to us all. That might be a devastating cancer diagnosis, a bereavement, the loss of a job or something else. But we don't become brave by staying in our comfort zones. We become brave by facing the pain, working through it and settling into our new normal.

Acknowledgements

I am blessed to have hundreds of people I could thank on these pages.

My whole family is so special to me. First off, Mum. This whole book is one big tribute to how you cared and sacrificed for me in those days. I am so grateful for you, and proud to have you as both my mum and my best friend.

To my sisters, Lauren and Georgia, who are also my best friends. I've always looked up to you both. Thanks for being my biggest supporters. It couldn't have been easy living in a household where your poorly sister took up so much of the attention, but thank you for persevering and supporting me at every turn.

Thank you to Georgia and Lauren's partners for being a part of our family, I'm glad my sisters have you both. And my gorgeous nephews and nieces, I love you more than words can say. I can't wait until you're old enough to read this book.

To Dad, for all the support you've offered during this terrible rollercoaster ride. Thank you for being my biggest cheerleader with all the work I'm doing now. Thanks for always being there.

I would also like to thank my stepdad, John. I love you so much. Even though you only came into my life when I went into remission, you've been my rock through some of the darker days of my recovery. It takes a lot to walk into a woman's life when she has three daughters and take on part of the parenting.

When I get married, I'll be lucky enough to have two dads walk me down the aisle, and I am blessed to have them both.

To Kaito, my absolute world. I pray you grow up to put kindness first and that you have the gentleness of your dad. Everything I do, I do with you and your future in mind.

To Max, the man who has never judged me, who is just as happy to see me walking around in my sweats without my prosthetic eye

110

as when I'm all glammed up for a night out. Thank you for being such a supportive partner.

To Nan and Grandad. You have been such a huge part of my life, including my treatment and recovery. Thank you for every hospital trip, every prayer and every kind word. You're my second parents, and I don't know where I'd be without you.

To those who will sadly never get the chance to read this book: my great-nan and great-grandad, and my dad's parents. I am comforted to know that you are looking out for me and cheering me on from up there.

To my cousin Claudia for delivering my baby, to my cousin Lewis for messing around with my wigs and making me laugh when I didn't think I had any laughter left in me. All of my aunties and uncles are so special to me. They've been so kind and supportive. Special thanks to Auntie Mandy and Uncle Chris for always lifting me up when I felt low and down on myself. To Zoe, Lauren's best friend, who is about to marry Uncle Chris. It's a real pleasure to have you in our family, and thanks for being there through all the highs and lows. We couldn't ask for a better wife for Uncle Chris. And then there's Ian, Zoe's husband. What an incredible partner you are. You are truly part of the family.

Thanks also to my wonderful friends – those who are mentioned in this book and those who aren't. My cousin Megan, who falls into both the friend and family category, Nicole, Lou, Lily, Elisha, Meg, Michael, Oran and Mia. Where would I be without the friendship you have shown me over the years? Being in your company makes every moment better. You've been there from the start, and I hope we continue to cheer each other on for the rest of our lives.

I'd also love to mention Harriet, Anya, Connor and Oli, who aren't regularly in my life any more, as people drift over time. But I will never forget the kindness you showed me or the impact you had on my life. You were there when I needed you, and it meant the world. And thanks to Dana, Harriet, Meg and Nicole for being such incredible friends during my diagnosis and treatment.

To every person who was involved in my care – you are amazing. Supporting children through such dark times can take it out of you, but each of you gave so generously to me and my family. It moves me every time I think about it. To Mr Hungerford, Dr Kingston, Mr Ready, Mr Sagoo, Laura, Tera, Dawn and Leslie. You treat people all the time, and in time you may forget me, but I will never forget you. You saved my life, and there are no words I can find to adequately thank you for that.

A massive thank you to Katie Piper. I wouldn't have written this book if it hadn't been for your encouragement. Thank you for relentlessly championing me, and for believing that my story was worth telling. I am forever in your debt.

I'm also so grateful to the team at SPCK, and to my editorial consultant Lauren Windle for helping me achieve my dream of writing a book and supporting me through the writing journey.

And finally, thank you to God, for keeping me safe, hearing my prayers, and bringing me a life and family beyond my wildest dreams.